HOW DO I ESCAPE
WHEN I'M TRAPPED IN
MY OWN MIND ?

HOW DO I ESCAPE
WHEN I'M TRAPPED IN
MY OWN MIND?

KRIS JONES

iUniverse, Inc.
Bloomington

HOW DO I ESCAPE WHEN I'M TRAPPED IN MY OWN MIND?

iUniverse books may be ordered through booksellers or by contacting:

iUniverse
1663 Liberty Drive
Bloomington, IN 47403
www.iuniverse.com
1-800-Authors (1-800-288-4677)

ISBN: 978-1-4620-3564-9 (sc)
ISBN: 978-1-4620-3566-3 (dj)
ISBN: 978-1-4620-3565-6 (ebk)

Printed in the United States of America

iUniverse rev. date: 07/07/2011

*F*or almost eight years I have been imprisoned emotionally mentally and spiritually. With every trial and tribulation the sentencing became more and more unbearable. Many individual's become discombobulated at the sight of being imprisoned in a small 4 by 3 jail cell. In writing this book I intend to over turn my prison sentence and set myself free. I would like to dedicate this book to the memory of my mother Maxine Jones, who departed her life Tuesday morning February 5, 2002. She taught me to be independent, hardworking and always strive to do your best. I love you, and miss you. You will never be forgotten. Rest in Peace

Chapter 1

The Beginning

*I*t all started one fall day in November; the year was 1998. It was supposed to be just like any other day. Mom woke up early to take the two foster children that were in our home to school, then coming back to walk me to my bus stop. Our ordinary routine changed and it changed my life forever. While mom was eating a bowl of cereal she looked at her swollen right arm and said, "This is a sign of a stroke", she then started to rub alcohol on her arm. I don't know if the alcohol spade the process of the stroke, but with—in minutes her right side started to give out. I was only 14 at the time so I really didn't know what to do' my first insist was to get her back in the house and call 911. That wasn't an option. My mother felt like there was roots put on the house, so all she kept repeating was get me out of this house.

Once we were out of the house and at the bottom of the stairs one of the drug dealers from the neighbor hood asked Miss Maxine what's the matter? She couldn't really answer him, but she grabbed his arm so tight and wouldn't let it go' it scared the living day lights out of him. He was so afraid he jumped in his car and drove up to my older sister's house and notified them of what was happening. Once we were outside mom said, "get me away from this house walk me to the corner", I said mom you can barley walk, but she was determined to get herself as far away as possible.

Someone screamed out what's wrong? I stated my mother was having a stroke and asked could they call 911. While we waited I begin to freak out. Why is it taking so long for the ambulance to come? Mean while my mother's eyes were changing. I can't explain it but every second we waited it looked as though her features were changing more and more. Now that I'm older I realized while we were waiting she had two severe strokes and two seizures. Since we were living in a drug infected area it took a total of three maybe four calls before the ambulance finally arrived. If we had called in and said," there's someone dealing drugs in front of my house the police would have been there within minutes.

Once inside the ambulance, they begin to ask me several questions, questions that I probably could have been able to answer if we were in a different situation.

At least some of them, what's your mother's birthday, do you know her social, what health problems does she have. As they were asking me questions the only thing that kept running through my mind was if my sisters would be at the hospital when we got there. I was so relieved when we got to the hospital to find my older sisters Debbie and Monica sitting in the hospital emergency room waiting for.

They doctors started to cut my mother's clothes off of her so they would be able to administer the medical care she needed. My sister's broke down at the sight of seeing my mother, in that stage all she was able to do was move her head from side to side moan.

Within hours of being at the hospital my mother slipped into a coma, the doctor's told us to be ready for anything because after having two strokes and a seizure she wouldn't survive and even if she did she would be a vegetable. Meaning she would need someone to care for her for the rest of her life.

Though my mother was in the hospital and we all wanted to stay with her, we had two foster children we needed to break the news to. We had to tell them that mom was sick in the hospital, and she might not get any better. Monica and Debbie called our father and some other family relatives so that they would have someone around to kind of keep them trucking forward. Debbie decided she was the oldest and since Monica had a four year old daughter she would put a hold on her acting and modeling career to take care of the foster children and myself.

Some, how that idea was short lived' within week's maybe even a month the children's social work knocked on the door. He stated," Deb I know that you have been taking the classes to become a foster parent but I'm sorry to inform you that I have to remove the children from your home. In amazement Deb asked him why? The children are happy with me and I take great care of them. He told us that someone you know called in and said that you were unfit to raise the children. You also had men running in and out of the house.

We were dumb founded. Who would say such a lie? Then, Deb remembered there was a lady at the church who said she wanted the children.

When Deb phoned her she stated, "Yeah I called them, what you going to do about it, you can't whop no body." Deb and I looked at each other and fell out laughing. What kind of mess is that? Since foster care removed the children from the home it was just Deb and I.

I was a freshman at Paterson Catholic H.S when my mother had her stroke. My sister tried her best to let me continue my education at PC but with the cost of tuition, and other necessities we needed at home that was starting to look undoable. My sister decided to enroll me in to East

Side High School. That was a major change for me, going from being in a school of only four hundred students to a big school like East Side.

Being at Eastside High led me to do and see things I never done before, like cutting class, seeing my teachers fight students. Those same teachers that taught me in class were some of the same people buying drugs almost right in front of my house. One Afternoon while I was walking to school, I observed my math teacher buying crack from one of drug dealers on my block.

That's when I realized I needed to do whatever I had to, to get back into Paterson Catholic. I really don't know how the school allowed me but within two months I was back walking the halls and taking classes at PC. After about two weeks of being in a coma mom finally awoke, the two strokes mom had paralyzed her left side and she needed to be cared for just like the doctor stated. When mom was released she was giving a hospital bed, and other necessities to help us care for her. After about a month or so, things were finally starting to get better. At first it was a little difficult to take care of mom but we all tried to stick together, some days we didn't know whether we were coming or going. After mom had been home for about a month or two, everything started to feel like a daily routine.

Just when I thought things were getting better my grandmother was rushed to the hospital, she had a stroke in her sleep and sometime after slipped into a coma. My grandmother Charlene Smith God rest in peace was called home February 16, 2000. Her death took the breath out of each and every family member. She was the glue that held the family together. After my grandmother died some days my sister and I didn't want to get out of bed but we knew we had to care for mommy.

Chapter 2

Just When the Sun Started to Shine

*I*t was hard being a 15 year old student in the morning and by afternoon working for different friends of the family then coming home and helping my sisters take care of my paralyzed mother. I hated coming home and seeing my older sister struggling trying to buy food for us and other things we needed for mom. Watching the drug dealers outside made me want to make fast money to help my family out of the bind we were in.

One afternoon one of the drug dealers from my neighbor hood approached me with work and I accepted it. I soon noticed that when it was time to pay me he would make up excuses so I decided to go in to business for myself.

Our house was in a position on a perfect angle that I was able to see all around the neighborhood. I would put in work earlier in the morning because Deb was either sleeping or at work. For some reason the drug dealers never told my sister even though they were cool with her. She was even dating two of them. Maybe it's because they under stood what I was going through and how I really need the money.

The money was enough to pay my tuition plus buy food for the house and any other things we might have needed. Any time Deb asked me where I was getting the money from, I would always lie and say the guys outside give it to me. She actually believed me. That was only because we were really cool with the drug dealers and at times they would give us a few dollars just to help us out.

One day I came home from school. Deb said, Kris, I went to pay your tuition thinking I was doing something. I had my fur coat on and the lady said mama it's already been paid. She said I didn't even ask her too much sure, I just left right out the door with my money still in my pocket.

I wanted to say that's because I had already paid the school but I didn't. I just looked at her and started laughing and couldn't stop. One day I brought a product that was too much for me to handle so I went to my father thinking that he would be able to help. Why I went to him, I may never really know. All I can say is within a few days he gave me a bullshit story how this guy hustled him. Negro please, my father is 6'5 300 and some odd pounds with a really bad and fucked up temper. I have yet to know a man that has crossed him.

Chapter 3

Paying the Price

*A*lmost at the end of my sophomore year Debbie decided she wanted to move back to Virginia. She told me either I could move with her or I could stay with daddy.

When I asked what about mom, she said mom wanted to go to South Carolina and be with some of her old church friends. I didn't want to move to Virginia since I had just enrolled myself back into school but at the same time I didn't want to move with my father.

The only reason I moved with him is my mother before she had her stoke worked two jobs for me to go to Paterson Catholic. Everyone in my family graduated from Kennedy High School, she just wanted me to be different and I didn't want to let her down.

I couldn't stay with Monica because she had a one bedroom apartment for her and her five year old daughter. People would always say you can come and stay with me but when ever I would take them up on their offer they would renege and change their minds. So the only choice I had was staying with my father. I was hoping the gut feeling I had about staying with dad was wrong. But within a few days I realized my instincts was correct. Don't remember exactly but a short time after I moved in my father started to molest me.

He would always tell me you have no where else to go, and the truth is I didn't. Any time I wanted to go places or to do anything he would always say I had a price to pay. By the mid or beginning summer my younger brother came to stay with us. I was so glad and relieved because I knew my father wouldn't be able to molest me any longer. Also it was good to be around my brother; ever since we were younger we would see each other once in a blue moon.

My brother was supposed to start school near where we lived. Then out of no-where his mother decided she was coming to pick up him. I was devastated when I heard he was leaving not just because I would miss him but I didn't want to be alone with my father again.

For sometime now I wanted to tell someone but who would believe me, everyone looked at my father like he was a king. At this point I didn't care any more. I just wanted out like an abused wife.

Chapter 4

Confronting My Family

One day I was hanging out with my sister's brother-in-law Kasey I asked him, if something every happed and I didn't have any where to go could I live with him and he said sure. Then he kind of looked at me and said why wants wrong, when I told him about my father he said I'm taking you down to the police station now. My heart was racing, I didn't know how my family was going to respond to me or the news of what my father was doing. Once down town I was introduced to someone who was going to take my statement and a prosecutor name Danny White who I will never forget.

After he took my statement Danny told me they were sending someone down to pick up my father but they were going to give him a story saying I ran away. At the point I was thinking my family is going to kill me for what I had done. But I knew it was too late to turn back. I was definitely going to feel the warm and steamy wrath of my family. Once they picked up my father and had him in the office they insisted I needed to call someone to explain what was going on and for them to pick me up.

The only person that I had to call was my sister Monica but I knew she was going to kill me. When I called her she immediately asked me where was I? She must have looked at her caller ID. Next thing I know she was screaming, what you doing at the prosecutor's office.

They came to grammas house and picked daddy up saying you ran away get out of there before you get him in trouble. From everything that was going on all I could do was just beat my head and my hand on the way. Any time I felt stressed and I couldn't handle what was going on, I would hit me head or my hand against the wall or anything hard. Danny immediately took the phone and asked my sister what was going on? Before she could get a word in he said your father just admitted to every single thing your sister accused him of. My father told him he never considered me to be his daughter. When Danny said that, I actually thought back to when I was a child, my mother told me that when I was baby my father denied me as his child.

Now that I'm older I think about that and laugh. I'm the only one of my father's kids that is actually built like him and look extremely like him. Debbie always laughs and says for a female you have very broad shoulders. I guess that was god's funny way of proving to my dad I am his child.

Monica asked Danny could she call my older sister Debbie and put them on a three way so Deb would be able to know what's going on. After explaining the process to my sisters of what was going to happen next, he Okayed her to pick me up.

Once I was in the car with Monica I jumped down in the seat and docked at the sight of seeing a van that was similar to my fathers. Even though he was locked up I thought maybe some how he conned his way out of it just like he did everything else, and they released him. Monica didn't say anything but I knew that first place she was going to take me was either my Aunt Latoya or my Aunt Melinda. I know that the family had their own comments and questions that they wanted to approach me with. All I could do was be honest. The hardest part was over. At least I thought it was over.

The first person that Monica took me too was my Aunt Latoya, to my surprise she didn't scull me on what was going he reported me father. She said," I know that he's my brother but what he did was wrong he doesn't need to be in jail he needs to be under the jail." The next stop we made was to my grandmother's house. I knew that things weren't going to go as smooth there as they did with Aunt Latoya. When I got there my two uncles Lass and Dale were sitting outside on the porch. They didn't say anything. They just kind of looked at me. Maybe they wanted to say something but they didn't know what to say. Once inside of the house my Aunt Melinda and Aunt Destiny along with my grandfather were there to question me and make their own comments.

They wanted to know why I didn't tell them. Why did I tell Kasey, even after I told Kasey why he didn't come to them instead of taking me downtown to the police station? My family felt that now everyone was going to be in their business and is going to know what my father did. We could have handled the situation without it even leaving the family. With in minutes of talking to my family and explaining to them what happen, my younger brother came into the house. He asked me what happen and why didn't I tell him. My answer was simple and short. I didn't think anyone was going to believe. Imagine if daddy denied everything I said, who was going to believe me and who would be on my side.

Of course my brother said he would believe me. We hugged, kissed and said we loved each other and was going to try and keep in touch. After talking to my family I knew the next thing I had to worry about was where I was going to stay.

Chapter 5

Finding Other Living Arrangements

I still didn't want to move to Virginia but I knew Monica was only going to let me stay with her a few nights. My older cousins had an apartment not too far away from where I was staying with my father; I figured maybe I could stay with them for awhile. I never stopped to think the entire process through. Meaning once I told what my father was doing to me, who all would find out.

It seemed like just a day later and people seem to already know. One of Debbie's old boyfriends Curtis, who lived right across from my cousin's seen me outside and started to stare at me. Curtis and Deb had dated some years back and Curt was like my big brother.

Curt Finally walked over and said," Krystal what's wrong what's the matter?" Before I could say anything my cousin answered and said nothing Curtis. He kind of gave her a look, like I'm talking to her not you. So I just looked up at him and said no nothing, I'm ok. I wasn't comfortable and ready to repeat the entire story over and over again. With in a few days my father made bail. I wasn't surprised I knew he would. My worst nightmare was my family taking me to him and saying we're going to handle this on our own. Don't get me wrong I wasn't afraid because I lied, I told the honest truth. I was afraid like a rape victim seeing her attacker face to face. You're afraid of what he might do to you next now that he knows you reported him.

A few months after mom moved to South Carolina with her church friends she decided she wanted to come back to New Jersey. I guess it wasn't what she thought it would be or she just missed her own family. After moving back to Jersey mom started staying with Monica.

School was starting soon and I had no idea where I was going to live. My godmother told me I could stay with her, but then changed her mind when someone told her don't let that girl stay with you and ruining your family like she did ours. I went back to Kasey and asked could I stay with him? Poor Kasey, my family had already begun jumping down on him. They would call and scream at him saying who do you think you are, taking her down to the police station; you should have brought her to one of us. Since Kasey wasn't completely stable his mother and her long time boyfriend agreed to take me in.

I didn't know then but I was going to have so much drama staying with my sister's soon to be ex-in-laws.

Chapter 6

A Whole New Set of Drama

*E*verything started out good. I even had my own room; I was finally living in a comfortable environment again. Jeffery, Kasey older brother who was Monica's soon to be ex-husband was now going to be my foster brother.

He even introduced me to his girlfriend and his three year old son. Before you know it I was hanging with Jeffery's girlfriend. She even introduced me to her family.

After a while I started hanging with her and her family. They thought I was pretty cool and down to earth for being the ex-wife's sister. Little did I know things were going to change and they weren't going to change for the best. My first Christmas with the new family seemed ok until Monica came to drop my niece off with her father. She decided she wanted to go up stairs and snoop around Jeffery's room, to see if he was being honest with his income. Next thing I know she came down stairs and she wasn't happy. Before long incidents like that, were occurring almost once a week. One day while I was watching TV. A gentleman came to serve Jeffery his divorce paper but since he wasn't home, I signed for them.

Think about how odd I felt signing for sister's divorce papers. That's nothing compared to the drama and bullshit trucking ahead. Pretty soon Mrs. Thompson and Robert started calling me their daughter. Kasey and Jeffery started calling me their little sister.

Before I knew it school was about to begin, Mrs. Thompson took me school shopping to get a few new uniforms for school and a few other things. My life was totally the opposite of what it was with my mother. At times with mother we walked all over god's creation. She never once would stop to ask anyone for a ride. She would always say, "They see us walking if they wanted to give us a ride they would stop and offer." There were five other people that stayed in the house at times and they all drove. Meaning I didn't have to walk unless I wanted too.

A little while after school started I was faced with going to court for the molestation case against my father. Debbie and Kasey were the only two people that went to court with me. While in court my father tried to con his way free by reciting bible verses and trying to put on his man of God act.

It didn't work not one bit. The prosecutor saw right through his bullshit. He even asked, "Mr. Smith can you show me where in the bible it says it's ok to molest your own child."

My father was speechless. The judge ordered him to start serving his time immediately; he was taken into jail that very day. I was ordered to mandatory counseling at a local hospital one day a week. Even though the counseling was mandatory, I stop going after a few weeks.

The sessions were doing more harm than good. I started hitting my hand more frequent, and the more I hit it they harder I hit it. They were times in school where I had to leave class because everything was so over whelming. A few weeks after court Jeffery asked me if I wanted to ride with him in his truck bed while he was working to keep him company. I agreed.

I though it would be fun to ride in a big truck that had a TV and bed in it. Once way got back he pulled over to a safe distance on side of the road. Jeffery said," I need to talk to you." The way he looked at me I knew it was serious. He told me Curtis, Debbie's old boyfriend was shot and killed. I couldn't believe it. Who would want to kill him and why? I was emotionless for a brief second, but I knew the way I was feeling was nothing compared to the way Debbie would feel. When I told her she just started breaking down and couldn't compose herself.

Chapter 7

Oh God Why Me?

A little while after mom moved in with Monica she started falling a lot and all the progress she made from rehabilitation started to decrease more and more. Monica decided to take mommy to the hospital to find out exactly what was going on.

But like doctors they have to know what they're looking for to be able find something. After the doctors couldn't find anything they sent her home. A little while after mom was sent home she started to bleed vaginally like she had a menstrual cycle. Once at the hospital Monica was notified that my mother had ovarian cancer. She was also told mom was in her last stages and she had only six months to live.

I still remember the night Monica, Debbie and the rest of the family told me the news. We were all at my grandmother's one dark night in November; they asked me to step outside. While outside they slowly broke the news to be bit by bit.

I couldn't believe my ears, I felt like the entire world was falling apart. I entered in freshman year with mom getting sick and here it is my senior year I would end at her funeral. While mom was in the hospital I tried to spend as much time with her as possible but it was beginning to get harder and harder. The cancer was started to spread and eat away at her brain, so sometimes she didn't even know I was there. One night I went to visit her she had tubes in her nose and in her mouth. Out of no-where she pulled one of the tubes out of her nose. I couldn't do anything but call Monica and cry. It was hard seeing my mother in the stage she was in. At one point the cancer ate away so much of her brain when she would be in pain she would just moan and shake her head from side to side. Whenever we would ask her where the pain was at, she wouldn't response just moan

One day while I was in gym, I felt a cold chill over my body. I told one of my friends that something was wrong at the hospital, I just didn't feel right. She replied," If something was wrong your family would come to get you from school. Stop worrying everything is ok." At the beginning of my next period class, my vice principal knocked on the door and asked for me. She said, "Someone is claiming to be your uncle and he asked to see you." While walking down the hallway to her office I felt like an inmate on death row about to be executed. I had already known who the man was, not only that I knew why he was coming to get me.

My family had to send a man to come and escort me to the hospital because they knew I was going to flip. They needed someone who could handle my anger and me lashing out.

Once we got to my Uncle I just looked at him and said," Uncle Lass what happened at the hospital. All he could do was raise his hand and say baby, I'm sorry your mom died this morning. Even though I already knew she was gone, but just hearing the worst took my feet right from under me. I fall to the ground. I couldn't believe it. My mother was gone. She died the morning off February 5, 2002.

After a few minutes of consoling and talking to me, he said everyone is waiting for you at the hospital. I rushed to my locker got my things and walked out the door.

When we arrived to the hospital Monica, Debbie; my Aunt Melinda and the rest of our family and friends were there ready to console me. But just at the sight of seeing my mother's life less body led me to lash out and start screaming now, "I'm all alone I don't have anyone." My family started hugging me saying don't feel like that, you have us your not alone. The sight of seeing my mom's body was too much for me to handle, I decided to go into the bathroom and beat my hand. I banged on the wall until the pain left me motionless. My older cousins thought it would be a good idea to leave the hospital, so the last memory I have of my mom would not be her deceased body.

Chapter 8

Trying To Cope
With My Mother's Death

*A*fter the morgue came to pick up my mothers body the entire family decided to go to Monica's house and have a few drinks. Any time that our family experienced death, we would always, laugh have fun and have a few drinks. Some people would say that sounds like alcoholics to me, but that's the way we handled losing a love one. At the time of my mother's death I was 17 years old. It didn't matter whether I was 7, 17, or 37; I still needed and wanted my mom.

My mom's siblings came up from South Carolina along with their children for the, funeral procession but some of them had other things on their mind other than paying their respect. My mother's brother Larry asked, could he talk to my sister Monica out in the hallway. I don't know what their discussion was but it only took about 10 minutes. Some of my friends from school and a company called Rail Road Construction come to my mom's funeral on my behalf. They even sent flowers and a card with money inside of it. As soon as my family and I stepped inside of the church I felt my lungs collapsing. I started to freak out and have an acute panic attack. Debbie being the oldest decided to take me to the bathroom and try to calm me down. She said, Krystal don't start acting crazy, I know it's hard but try to keep it together.

People just didn't realize, all my life it was just me and my mother, and now that she's gone I would spend the rest of my life alone no matter how much family I have. Things will never be the same.

After returning to my seat I kept my composure as long as I could. Before I knew it I was breaking down and crying the hardest I have ever cried before. My godmother's and other people tried to console me, but I screamed leave me alone!!!!! As far as I was concerned, there was nothing they could have said to take the pain away. My Aunt Melinda's husband minister Dale Thomas preached my mother's home going service. I felt like he was the only one who understood exactly what I was feeling. In the eulogy he stated that no matter what anyone would say to my mother and how big I got I was always her baby.

After service Monica and the rest of the family stayed to eat in the back of the church. While Debbie and I left to go to Monica's house and have drinks with Deb's boyfriend.

A little while later Monica her boyfriend Victor and our cousin's joined us at the house for a few drinks. While drinking Monica started to reminisce about mom and our grandmother, she just couldn't believe within two years they both were gone. One at a time we all tried to speak with cracking voices, but before long we were all in tears. Everyone decided that it was to depressing just sitting in the house. They decided to go to a sports bar. I decided to head home, just wanted to be by myself. That next morning Monica called me and asked was I going to the burial sight, I declined. I didn't think I could handle them lowering my mother into her final resting place. Monica agreed and said we would see you later.

A few days passed and Mrs. Thompson told me I had to go back to school. I didn't feel like I was ready but she told me, sitting around would only make things worse. Going back to school I felt like everyone was watching, trying to see how I would react after losing my mother. Finally after a few days, things started to go back to normal. What every, you consider normal to be.

Chapter 9

Monica and Jeffery

*T*he drama with Monica and Jeffery was only getting worse by the day. Some days Monica and I would argue because she felt I was hanging and being friends with the woman who broke up her marriage, even though Monica was living with her boyfriend.

I tried to explain these people took me in when no one else wanted me; I can't just be mean to her and her family. On top of that sometimes she does more for me than you do. If I ask you for money you say ask her, when I ask her you get pissed at me.

With all the drama, losing my mother and grandmother I felt like my world was crumbling at my feet. I couldn't take it any more. I decided to take a few pills and drink some rubbing alcohol that was from under the sink. I felt for sure the two combined would surely do the trick. I tried to call my sisters and to tell them what was going on but could not reach them. Finally I called my Aunt Latoya she came over to talk to me and took me home with her. The pills and alcohol didn't kill me. It just made me sick.

Since it was my senior year, I was busy filling out college applications and getting ready for prom. Even though Monica and I had our problems she said she would pay for me to have my own limo. I thought it was kind of cool and also nice for her to say that. My family loved to dress up and all agreed they would do my hair and make up. We even had a dress rehearsal of how everything would go. Mrs. Thompson and Robert paid for my dress and shoes. My dress was black with silver dots in it; I don't really remember what color my shoes were.

A few weeks before prom, I received a letter in the mail that I was accepted to Kean University EEO program.

The day of my prom everyone came over to Mrs. Thompson house to get me ready for the prom. Vicki who is my Aunt Melinda oldest daughter did my hair. Dawn who is my cousin and god sister did my makeup and eye brows. What's funny is my Uncle Lass, who is my Aunt Latoya's boyfriend. He was even there. He shaped my edges up so they wouldn't look bad.

Monica and Debbie were upstairs helping me to get dressed; my family took great pride and enjoyment in my prom, since I was going to be the last female to graduate high school for a few years. Once it was time for us to leave, I saw my entire family outside. Cousin slash god sister Stephanie, Victor, even Debbie's boyfriend was there.

My family followed us half way to the prom so they wouldn't miss anything. At the time of my prom I was dating this guy name Keith, so I took him to the prom with me. My friend Martina, Clarence and a girl name Sabrina from school rode in the limo with me. Everything was nice but I really wasn't enjoying myself. Shortly after arriving at the prom I was ready to go. Keith wanted to ride around and go to New York but I just wanted to go home. He was a nice guy and at times I was in love with him and at times I didn't care how I treated him. Every time I dated a guy my family would always say, he's nice. Why are you so hard on him?

The next morning, Aunt Melinda, my cousin Rebie and Michelle where at the house wanting to know exactly what happened at the prom. I explained I wasn't having fun so I just left. They called me a party pooper and said I should have stayed. Since my graduation was June 1, 2002, Mrs. Thompson paid for me to go to a local hair dresser and have my hair done. That next morning I was so nervous, I wanted everything to go exactly the way my class and I had been practicing. Almost everyone was at my graduation. Aunt Melinda, Michelle, Vicki, Aunt Latoya, Monica, Debbie, Uncle Calvin, Jeffery girlfriend and her sister. Mrs. Thompson and Robert even video tapped the graduation I believed.

Pretty soon all the excitement of graduation was over, within a few days I was actually in Kean's summer program. The program was for students who either did poorly in school or on their SAT's. They had a great program; they were very hands on with their student tutoring programs, they even had freshman counselors'. It was a month or so program to get us ready for the fall semester, so we wouldn't have any problems switching from high school to college students.

After the program was over the counselors treated each and every student to some find and wonderful experiences. I had the honor of seeing a play featuring Vanessa Williams. We were even taken on the New York City Spirit Cruise that went around ground zero and other parts of NYC.

Chapter 10

Mom's Insurance Money

Once back home Monica and I really started to bump heads, we started to argue more and more each time. One night while we were all sitting outside at my grandmother's house I asked Monica about mom's insurance check. She explained we weren't getting it until October and don't worry about it, when I get it I'll give you some.

I started to ask questions like why October, and was the policy in my name? It was a little odd to me that we had to wait until October, which was when I would turn 18. After talking to a few people they help me put the pieces together. They explained the policy was in my name and that was the only reason she had to wait till October. I was instructed to talk to my Uncle Rodney my mother's brother who she spent some time with in S. Carolina. When speaking to him I explained that the policy was in my name. Monica or he had no business signing on my behalf and I wasn't going to sign for him but I would give him something after I received the money.

He agreed and gave me all the information I needed to get the insurance check. As days went by Monica really started to show her ass in front of my Aunt Latoya and other family members. Until one day I shouted, you think you're slick that policy was for me to start school maybe even get a cheap car. Mommy felt you and Debbie were grown and she left the money to me. Monica quickly got defensive and said no it's not, I helped pay for mommy's funeral I'm taking what I want out and splitting the rest with you and Deb.

I quickly explained I already contacted the insurance company. She then jumped up and said now, its going to take forever for us to get the money you messed up listening to other people. She felt dumb when I told her I spoke to the insurance agent, and let her know I'm 18 and I wanted to collect the money myself. I informed Monica the agent also said well being that your 18 I'm going to throw your sister's paper work in the garbage because she has no access to it since it's in your name.

With school about to start back I tried to focus all of my anger and frustration towards my classes. It was a little difficult since I declined housing to save money, every morning I had to get up about 5 or 6 just to be at to school on time. The ride wasn't too bad since I had my cousin Sarah going to the same school; we were even in a few of the same classes.

A few times I fell asleep on the bus, and would have to ride until the last stop making me late for class. As time were getting closer and closer to my 18 birthday Monica would call and harass me, saying I was the one who paid for mom's funeral not you or Debbie I should be reimbursed.

She would always say I was planning on buying a truck with my tax return but instead I was the one who paid for mommy's expenses. I called Debbie and told her I was planning on sharing the money with her but wasn't giving Monica a damn thing. Debbie not wanting to piss me off agreed and said it's your money you do what you want.

At times the stress of school and arguing with Monica was getting so over whelmed, I called her and said what if I killed myself how would you get the money then. Deb's boyfriend seeing how stressed I was, decided to talk to me. He explained you guys are all you have; don't let a few dollars get in between you and your sisters. Sit down and talk to them. Maybe even say to Monica, look we can split the money. What you do with your half is your business.

I totally agreed with him and decided to talk to Monica. Monica was fine with splitting the money three ways, but then I asked if we split the money how we would give Uncle Rodney any of the insurance check. Monica really didn't care as long as she had her half. Once the check arrived I called Monica and Deb so that we could go to the bank and spilt the money. After depositing the money for a few days, the bank manager pulled me aside and asked was I sure I wanted to split the money with my sisters.

He even asked were they threatening me of any kind, and felt I should take a few days to think everything over. I explained I wanted to share the money with them because it was the right thing to do. Moments after leaving the bank, I began to get phone calls from family and friends. Telling me what they were going through, hopping I would give them some of the money. My sisters and I went shopping, out to eat and anything else you could think of. I even tried to keep my promise to my Uncle Rodney but the money I wanted to give him, wasn't good enough. He felt I should have split the money with him instead of Deb and Monica.

Chapter 11

Your 18 Now . . . You on your Own

*J*ust when things were getting better with Monica, I started having problems with my foster family. I don't know if they felt I should have shared it with them or used the money to move out. But things really started to go south and fast. Some days after school instead of going home I would just spend the night at Monica's. We would have fun just sitting back laughing and giggling and having a few drinks.

One day I got so sick with a bad cold that I was unable to go to school or even go home. A little while after I received a phone call from Robert he told me he heard I wasn't in school and if I wasn't going to school then I was not going to be living in their house.

I tried to explain that I was still in school but I was sick with a bad cold. For what every reason he did not want to hear what I was saying and eventually told me I had to move out of their house. I was devastated after hearing this news; I asked Monica could she call them and explain that I was really sick. Even when Monica called they did not want to hear what she was saying, in fact they told her they only reason she was calling because she didn't want me to move in with her.

Deb's boyfriend came up with the ideal why don't the two of you move into an apartment together. I agreed being that I didn't have any where else to go. When I arrived at Mrs. Thompson and Robert's house to get my things, Jeffery stopped me. He said he was told I was talking about him, stating I was going to get Monica's boyfriend to beat him up. I tried to assure him that I never made that comment but he just looked at me, like "yea whatever."

I tried to continue and buckle down to my school work but with everything going on I wasn't doing to well. I was left with no other choice but to speak to the president and the dean of the school. I explained what was going on with my foster family, my family and how I just lost my mom. The dean agreed and felt I jumped the gun when I enrolled into college. She felt I should have taken a year off after finishing high school.

Deb and I found a lovely but expensive two bedroom apartment in Lodi. The move cleaned both of us out. Deb enrolled in PCC College in downtown Paterson where she also applied for a work-study job.

I decided to get a job at the local grocery story called A&P. The job was ok at first. Bringing in 200 dollars a month plus every now and then I would steal groceries and bring them home. Our bills including rent, utilities and cable came to about 1400 a month.

We were so stressed with rent and work that we started to drink a lot; at least I know I did. The apartment was so expensive that we could not afford to buy furniture.

Deb's boyfriend got her a bed, I decided to take money out of my check and buy me a blow up bed. To think back even though we were stressed and tight with money living in Lodi was so much fun. We would have family get gatherings and birthday parties at the house. Everyone would call our place the hang out spot.

Since bills were beginning to pile up I decided the next time I was at work I was going to steal out of the register. That scam was cut short when my boss who was counting my register and said either the money shows up or he was going to call the police. After returning the money they asked, "Why did I try to steal", once I explain my situation they agreed not to call the police but told me I could not work there any more.

After I was let go I pondered how I was going to tell Debbie and how I was going to pay my half of the bills. A few days after I was fired a met someone online who agreed to help me. Every week he would send me 200 dollars like clock worth. So even though I wasn't working I was still bringing money into the house. The next problem I was faced with, was trying to make Deb believe I was still working. I would walk up and down route 46 East and west to pass time, stopping in different stores filling out job applications.

The first couple of days it was easy, but it was started to get colder and colder outside. One day I said fuck it, Deb I haven't been going to work I've been walking around trying to pass the time so you wouldn't know. She looked at her boyfriend and busted out laughing. She said, we knew you weren't working we just wanted to see how long you would walk your ass in the cold.

Her boyfriend said, take your ass in the kitchen and go have a drink. After a while I realized drinking took my pain and sorrows away. It made me forget any and everything I was going through. The landlord wasn't satisfied with us giving him 300 a week he wanted the entire 1200 at the beginning of the month.

We tried to explain it was impossible and we were trying our best to pay him his money. Within a few days we were told he was taking us to court to have is evicted.

Chapter 12

Cooking for New Start

I decided to reenroll in college. I remember there was a college in West Virginia who had been contacting me since my sophomore year in high school.

I knew it was going to be a process, and needed some where to stay until I had everything worked out. My cousin Vanessa agreed to let me stay with her for a little while. My friend online was still sending me 200 a week so I would be able to give her some money for staying with her. Debbie decided that she was going to more to North Carolina; a friend there said she would help Deb get on her feet. The stay with Vanessa was pretty cool; she had three kids so I was always entertained. I didn't stay with her too long. I traveled to Beckley, West Virginia April of 2003 to tour the college and fill out all of my necessary paper work and by May or June I was walking the college campus of Mountain State University.

It was pretty cool, I got to meet new people and for once in my life I got chance to be who I really wanted to be. I was able to act out things I had been feeling for years. Meaning I always wanted to be with a woman but was afraid of what my family might say if they knew I had gay tendencies. While enrolled at MOUNTAIN STATE UNIVERSITY in 03 I met and became good friends with a senior named Megan. She took me under her wings and showed me around campus. I was a little attracted to her so I would always push up on her, but she always declined saying where we were friends let's not mess up our friendship. She would always say, "Where would that leave us as friends?" You're my first real friend and I don't want us to mess up our friendship.

Megan would always try to drag me to different school functions and parties but I would always decline. I never really felt comfortable being around people. I always wanted to stay to myself. Within another week or so the fall semester started. I met a few other people CJ, Jason, Hector, Eric and a girl name Kristina. The way we bounded you would have thought we were friends for years. We had some much fun; we would go to Wal-Mart at two or three in the morning just to laugh and giggle to see who was in the store. They would always call CJ my boyfriend because we were always together. I guess CJ and I hung together because he was secretly into men and I was secretly into women. We were each others cover up.

When ever I would tell Megan about the woman I went with, she would say you know you're gay just come out of the closet, no one will look at you any differently. I would always answer and say "I'm not gay I just like the way pussy taste."

Now that I'm older and I think about that comment, I just laugh and say she was actually right. With all the fun I was having I should have kept up with my financial aid. I was notified with two months left in school that I had a balance, I was awarded work-study but it wasn't enough time to work my entire balance off. By November or December I was told that my balance was eight hundred dollars and they were not going to let me enroll for the next semester.

Once again I was faced with the dilemma where was I going to live. Debbie told me I should come down and stay with her. I would like it. I agreed and within a few days I was on a bus heading to Wilmington N.C.

Chapter 13

Drinking Accident at Deb's house

*T*he first few days I arrived everything was good, but I was starting to feel deep down inside that Debbie and I should not live together again. So after a few days of laughing giggling and drinking, I called Mrs. Thompson and asked could she pay for me a ticket to West Virginia and once there after I received my check I would pay her back.

She agreed but the ride to the bus station took so long when I get there the bus driver was already loaded and ready to go. He wouldn't even wait for me to get my ticket from the will-call ticket booth. He just left without me. How can you miss your bus when you're literally standing right next to it? I called my older brother Tyler and explained to help what was going on. He thought it would be a good ride to travel to N.C. then to West Virginia then back to NJ. We all had so much fun drinking and carrying on until we started drinking entirely too much.

Debbie started yelling and saying you're too grown for your own good you need to stay here with me instead of trying to do things on your own. She made some comments about my father molesting me and I made comments about the man that she was dating. The next thing I remember was grabbing a liter trying to set the house on fire by lighting her couches. I would always yell and say I don't have a reason to live. You don't have a reason to live. Let's just die right here and right now.

My brother Tyler grabbed the liter and tried to get me to calm down. Before long Deb started screamed "I want you to get her the fuck out of my house. I'm calling the police." I was so drunk I threw up all over the hallway stair wells.

When the police arrived Tyler explained it was just family arguing. We're actually leaving in the morning we can't leave tonight because I've been drinking. Debbie is leaving for work in about an hour or so I'm going to keep Kris out of the house until she leaves.

Debbie left for work eleven that night, just like Tyler told the police and we were on the road to West Virginia exactly seven that next morning. Once we arrived to West Virginia I was able to get a few of my checks and cash them so we would have gas money to return home to New Jersey. Looking back I don't know why I didn't just give the checks to the school who knows they probably would have let me register for the spring semester with a smaller balance. While in W.V we were hit with a big snow storm. Tyler decided we needed to get on the road before we were snowed in.

I said ok but I knew we would pay for it later. Tyler had only a few hours of sleep, he had been driving since seven the morning earlier, and we had another eight or nine hours more to drive before we were to reach New Jersey.

We got lost shortly after leaving W.V giving us an extra two or three hours to drive, Tyler started getting so tried that we literally had to pull over on the side of the highway because he couldn't keep his eyes open. He was afraid for me to drive, because I had just got my license and I have never drove on a highway or in the snow before. After another six or seven hour's we were finally in New Jersey because it was so late I decided to stay with Monica, but I knew I needed to make some living arrangements in the morning and fast.

Chapter 14

Reuniting With the Foster Family

*T*hat following morning I asked Mrs. Thompson could I stay with them just for a little while? She responded and said let me talk to Robert. After a few days they got back to me and said I can stay with them but I would have to sleep on the couch and I would have to find a job. I moved in a few days later and started looking for a job. At first everything was ok. Everyone in the family was cool; things seemed like they were when I was in high school. I started looking for jobs, but most jobs in the paper were scams or telemarketing places.

One afternoon Debbie called me and said I'm working in the human resource department at Kmart. Come down and I will give you a job. The job was kind of cool. The only thing I didn't like was the manager.

The manager was this guy name Fred who didn't know how to talk to people and treated them like shit. He would always ride my back about this or about that. Three weeks into working one afternoon Fred called me into his office, to bitch about me not doing a good job and if I didn't change he would fire me.

I kind of looked at him and smirked, because I knew he was being an asshole. A toddler just learning to walk could do my job. My job was picking things off the floor and returning them to their right department. Not hard. After his so called meeting I decided to take lunch and walk down to the nearest bar. After having a few drinks I said fuck Fred and that bitch ass job. I walked back in the building and told Debbie that I wasn't gong to kiss Scott's ass. I quit.

Debbie looked at me and said, I told you Fred was an asshole and I'll see you later. The next day I saw Debbie, she told me after I left Fred continued to call me over the p.a. system. He even called her asking if she had seen me. When she told him no, he said, well when you do tell her I said to come to my office.

I couldn't believe I was back at square one looking for another job, until I saw an ad in the paper looking for security guards. Since the job sounded legit I decided to follow up with it. A few weeks later I was working for a company called Allied Security; my first job sight was St. Joseph hospital in downtown Paterson.

The job was pretty cool; my duties were dispatching information to all officers on shift and documenting the information hour by hour. Most of all the officers got along, and the pay was also great, eight dollars an hour with plenty of overtime.

With the money I was making, I bought my first Vehicle, a Ford Explore. I also starting giving Robert and Mrs. Thompson a few dollars for letting me stay with them. Working at the job site was shortly lived, one afternoon there was an incident involving another worker. I followed protocol by calling the sight manger and documenting what time I called and what time he responded. He never responded, so to cover my ass I documented it in the login book and also called the one eight hundred number just like the protocol stated.

After staying with Robert and Mrs. Thompson, for about a few months, Jeffery came down stairs and said, "Why are you sleeping in the living room why don't you go and sleep in the basement". At first I thought it was a good idea, I would have my own privacy downstairs. No one to bother me, but the idea was shortly lived. Any time it would rain the basement would flood, any and every piece of article I had on the floor would be soaked by the time I came home from work.

A few days later when I returned to work my boss asked to see me in one of the offices. He told me he did not want me working for him, matter of fact he referred me to another sight that was a little further away but it was also a pretty neat job it wasn't like the hospital, but it was ok. I was working at William Paterson College signing students in and out of the Dormitories. Since it was a little farther I would either catch a ride with the school's transportation van or walk to work.

Some days I would drive half way and park the truck on a street that wasn't frequently filled with police. It was hard trying to give Robert and Mrs. Thompson money every week, plus trying to save money to get my own place. Therefore I was unable to purchases insurance to drive to and from work. With summer approaching my on sight supervisor informed me they were going to be only using two dormitories; therefore I would have to find a summer job. Kasey told me to consider trying to get my certified nurses assistance licenses, some places would pay you while your taking the CNA class, plus your guaranteed a job if you past the class.

Chapter 15

Bonded as a Family

*F*or once in my lifetime things were going ok. I had a pretty decent job, the pay wasn't great but it would lead to something long term. Every weekend the family and I would go out to either the Elks club or Masonic Temper. Depending on where Monica's boyfriend Victor would be working that weekend. He was a really big guy so they would use him for security, mean while we got in free. Even though we would go out for drinks every Friday and Saturday night, we would always make it to church no matter how much of a hangover we had in the morning.

After church we would all go out to eat at red lobster, change our clothes then head to the club. Now that I'm older, I realize we were drinking a lot because we all were going through something's but no one wanted to share. We were all involved in church functions, from the usher board to the church choir. Aunt Latoya even decided to start a youth praise dance team, that Vanessa and myself help run. Sometimes we would meet up at either Monica's or Aunt Latoya's house just to drink and have fun. But any time we did drink, something would always occur to cut the evening short. Either Victor would swear that Monica was flirting and make a fuss or Uncle Lass would say that Aunt Latoya was flirting and make a fuss.

Some nights I would get drunk and walk home. While walking home I would always punch bricks on different houses in frustration. Even though it had been a few years since mom passed and dad molested me I still had a lot of anger built up inside. I was starting to have problems with my truck, so I was forced to trade it in for a Mitsubishi galant. The payment on the car was about a hundred or so more dollars a month, so I kind of fall behind with paying Robert for rent. Since I was going to school during the day the only time I had to go out and hang with friends was at night. Jeffery would always say, "Why do you go out at night, you live and act like you're a prostitute."

About three or so weeks left of the c.n.a. classes my teacher pulled me and a few students over, and said you missed one class if you miss another class I will be forced to fail you. I tried to explain that I had been having vehicle problems and it would not happen again.

She was so nasty and not understanding that I just walked out of the office in frustration and said I quit. I felt like I was busting my ass for nothing, I mean damn they were only paying me six, forty-five an hour.

Even after the class I would only be making seven dollars an hour. With school now back in session, I was back to working my regular shift at William Paterson College.

Chapter 16

Down On My Luck

*S*ince the choir anniversary was right around the corner, I decided to go back to the nursing home and pick up my last check. When I arrived at the nursing home I was denied my paycheck because I hadn't returned all of my equipment. She said, "When you return your back brace we will mail you your check." I looked at her and said, "I didn't mail my work up in this motherfucker; you not about to mail me shit". Just when I was about to approach her, something inside of me said, "You're in a white neighbor they will arrest you right on the spot."

So I jumped back in the car and tried to retrace all of my steps, within a few hours I found the back brace in a local Burger King restaurant. Once I received my check I started shopping for different items for the choir anniversary. The anniversary fell on the sixteen of October which was the Saturday before my birthday; it turned out beautiful. I was running really late, I had to park the car and run to the front of the church, so that I would be able to march down the aisle with the rest of the choir.

A month after the anniversary the car dealer where I was buying my vehicle sent a repo truck to come and reprocess the car. It was so embarrassing Jeffery girlfriend and a few other people were at the house, so I knew that they were going to talk about me as soon as I left. I tried to talk to the car dealer and the repo man but since I was so far behind, he had no other choice but to take it. Seeing them pull of with my prize possession left me depressed and empty inside. I decided to walk to the liquor store for something to drink and clear my head. After a few drinks I decided that I would never ever make payments on a vehicle again.

It was hard walking when I was use to driving, but never the less I did want I had to, to get around. Robert starting riding my back more and more, I tried to explain that I didn't have any money and whenever I did I gave as much as I could. He didn't understand that most of the money I had was going into the car before they reposed it. My checks were only about five hundred every two weeks if that, and when I had the car I was paying two hundred and fifty a week. After gas, that left me with not even a dime in my pocket. Since I was making car payments anymore, I was able to give Robert three hundred a month and save the rest to buy a new vehicle.

After about a few weeks I was able to buy this Ford Explore It had a few problems; the gas hand didn't work so a few times I ran out of gas. But at the end of the day I didn't have to make any payments it was mine.

This time I wanted to make sure all the papers on the car were current, so instead of giving Robert money I would put money to the side to save. Things at home with them were starting to get so bad, that I would wait until they fell asleep before I walked into the house.

My grandmother's house around the corner was vacant, so I would either sit on the steps or park in front of the house with my seat so far back no one would see me sitting on there. I felt like every time I walked in the house they were always talking about me behind my back. There were days that I had to go to the bathroom but I would never come up stairs until I felt like no one was in the living room. One morning I woke up I decided instead of getting the papers right on the truck I would save money so that I would be able to get my own place. With that in mind I switched my job to a sight down route 287, the further the job the more they paid you.

Even though the job was far they paid ten dollars an hour, with little work to do. Since it had been a few weeks since I had given Robert any money he started calling my phone saying you can't stay here for free. Everyone contributes to something. I told him I understood but I was saving to get my own place. He told me he understood but if I was going to stay there I would have to give him something.

Chapter 17

DUI

*W*ith the stress from home and still having anger built up inside I started drinking more and more. I even started drinking and driving.

One night after work I stopped at a liquor store to pick up my favorite drink Como. After about my second can, I started filling a little buzzed so I decided to go ahead home. Before I got within a block to the house I was pulled over by a police officer, since I still had a can open I hide it under my seat. The police officer told me I almost cut an ambulance off, he saw that my eyes were blood shot red so he asked had I been drinking. I gave some bullshit story how I had been working since earlier that morning and just drove two hours from my job to get home.

He gave me a warning and told me to hurry up and get off of the road. After that close call I decided that I wasn't going to drink any more. I felt like that was God's way of warning me that something bad was about to happen. For about a month or so I didn't take not one sip of alcohol, the family would always laugh and say, let's see how long this is going to last. I would always joke and say, as long as I wanted it to.

The truth is it only lasted for about a month. New Years came and everyone had a drink instead of me. I was still holding to my pledge of not having any alcohol, until my Cousin Sarah's son Lamont's birthday. Sarah called me and said I'm giving the baby a birthday party come and hang out; you don't have to drink, just come and show your face. I told Sarah after work I would stop by and say hello I couldn't stay to long because I had to work the next morning. Once I got to Sarah's house I couldn't resist. I grabbed a can of Coors's light and starting drinking shot's of Paul Masion with my cousin Naim.

Debbie's boyfriend came over to the house to show his face but before he left he said, "Krystal don't drink and drive." You're going to end up with a "dui". Mark my word be careful. I hugged him and told him he had nothing to worry about I wasn't going to drive.

I don't really remember everything that happened that night. Deb told me that once we got to the kid's party I started drinking and acting a fool. She even said Kris you stepped in one of the kid's plate of cake. When someone told you, you cursed them out and said maybe they shouldn't be fucking eating on the floor. They told me even though I was stumbling around the house I continued to drink and disregard everything people were saying.

She told me pretty soon I couldn't even walk around the house but I was saying I was leaving. Deb said she remembers telling me, Kris if you drive that truck you're going to boil that shit up. She said I starting yelling and screaming that's my motherfucking, truck. If I want to boil it up then oh well. I paid for it with my motherfucking money.

After I left the birthday party, I don't really know what happen next, my cousin has his description of what happen and I have mine. The only thing I do remember is picking up a friend of mine and taking him to work, in the middle of taking him we got into a heated argument so I put him out. Thinking back, we were probably arguing because I was drunk and he was trying to tell me I shouldn't be drinking and driving

I remember on my way home getting pulled over by the police getting a ticket because the papers weren't right on my truck. Next thing I remember is having an accident; I don't even know why I was on that street. It was nowhere near my house.

Don't know what happen next, but I woke up in the police station with vomit all over my clothes. When I asked one of the police officers what happened he said, "You were drinking got into a bad accident, and was charged with a dui." They told me that at anytime I could go home, but they would only release me into someone else's custody. The only person I could reach was Aunt Latoya. I explained to her that I had been arrested and I needed her to come and get me. I asked the police officer where my truck was so that I could pick it up, he told me that it was totaled.

Whatever I hit, I hit it so hard I knocked the front axle off of the truck. After I was released I was told to report before the judge in the morning for a court date and If I did not appear a warrant would be put out for my arrest.

When Aunt Latoya took me to look at the truck I couldn't believe how badly it was. I literally wanted to cry. I had flushed all of my hard work down the drain, and not just that, how was I going to get to work. M job was about an hour or more down route 287. The next morning after hearing all of my charges in court I decided to tell the judge I wanted to get my own lawyer. Victor, Monica's boyfriend told me a friend of his was a lawyer. The lawyer owed him a favor so he would get him to take my case.

Mean while back at Mrs. Thompson house everyone was asking me what happen to my truck. I didn't want to hear what they had to say so I would always lie.

I told them the truck had been towed and since it was there for a few days it would cost more than I paid for the truck to get it out so I wasn't gong to bother. They probably knew more than they were letting on, but since they didn't say anything about the dui neither did I. After I told my supervisor what happen he told me it would be best if I worked at a sight that was close to where I lived.

Chapter 18

The Warrant

So within a week or two I was working at Bloomfield College. It wasn't far but it wasn't close. After my dui I realized that I was getting into too much trouble. I needed to get back in school fast. Since I only owned MOUNTAIN STATE UNIVERSITY eight hundred dollars, I mapped out a little to do list. The first thing on my list was to pay MOUNTAIN STATE UNIVERSITY so I would be able to attend school that summer. My plan was to work as much over time as possible to buy any and everything I needed for the travel to West Virginia. One morning while I was working I realized I was supposed to be in court. I called to reschedule but was told since it was a dui I could not. I was then notified that a warrant would be sent out for my arrest. Never once did I think twice about the warrant until one morning while I was sleeping the police came to the house looking for me.

That's when I decided I was going on the run, and I would continue to work until I was unable to. I packed a book bag full of cloths and stayed between my Aunt Latoya house and Vanessa house in East Orange. Some days I would even stay with students on the college campus. If I felt too tired to travel or if I thought the police were catching on to my where a bout, I would stay with other friends in Newark or Elizabeth. I went through this routine for about a month or so, maybe even a little longer. One afternoon while I was taking a nap I dreamed the police came to my job and arrested my on sight. When I awoke from my dream I quickly phoned my job and asked had anyone called looking for me.

The morning dispatcher said yes, "someone called asking if you were working tonight and what time was you coming in". Right then and there I knew what the police were planning, there were going to wait until I got nice and comfortable in my shift, then come to arrest me.

Within minutes I called the Paterson police department and asked, "what did I have to do to satisfy my warrant?" He told me I had to come down and turn myself in. Go before the judge to see if he would release me on my own recognizance or pay the thousand dollar bond. Once I got to the police station I was then notified, I had not one but two warrants for my arrest. One for Paterson and one for Ramsey, I was also told my bail was close to fifteen hundred dollars.

I tried to call Monica but she didn't answer so I then called Victor. I told Victor I was in jail and my bail was fifteen hundred dollars I needed to get out as soon as possible because I had to be at work by four o'clock

I also phoned my boss letting him know I was arrested and I would be late for work. He told me ok but to keep him posted. Since it was the first of April, April fool's day, Victor thought that I was joking and didn't call Monica for about an hour or so. It was starting to get late and I knew I wasn't going to make it to work for my four o'clock shift, so I started to get frustrated.

Within an hour or so of being locked up I started beating the walls until my knuckles turned pitch black just to get my mind off of work. I didn't know if my boss would fire me, and I needed the job to pay my balance at MOUNTAIN STATE UNIVERSITY. After about my third hour of being locked up, an officer came and said your family is trying to get up your bail money, they wanted to know how much money you had on you. After giving Robert money for staying with them I didn't have any money, but somehow some way my family hustled up the money.

Monica was able to borrow money from a few of our family members, assuring them that they would get their money back within a day or so. A thousand of the dollars was for me to reschedule my dui court cases and once I went to court that next morning they would return the money. The other five hundred I would have to repay the family out of my own pocket. Around seven o'clock I was told that my bail was posted and I was able to leave. The police officer who escorted me up stairs was an asshole; he wanted me to face the back wall the entire time we were on the elevator. I literally wanted to beat the shit out of him but I knew I had to hold my composure before I was taken back down stairs.

Once the elevator opened I was greeted by Monica, Victor, Aunt Latoya, Rebie and Uncle Dale. They asked me why was my hands so black, I told them I didn't have anything else to do so why not beat my hands on the wall.

The first think I did when I was released, was call my job. I really needed the hours so asked my boss was there any other shift I could work. He told me to come on in I could work the seven to three shift.

That was the coldest and longest day of my life. When I got off at three in the morning, there weren't any buses running so I was faced with walking home. That was the longest walk every, I walked from Bloomfield College to downtown Paterson. It took me approximately three hours or more to walk.

By the time I reached Monica's house on Slater St. my feet were burning and thumbing. They were hurting so bad I didn't even want them to touch each other.

Chapter 19

Getting Ready For The Travel

*A*fter working back to back overtime I finally had enough money to pay my balance off at MOUNTAIN STATE UNIVERSITY and buy other necessities I needed for the travel. I also applied for food stamps, I didn't know whether or not the café would be open but I wanted to be prepared. I gave my sight manger my two weeks notice. Letting him know I was going back to school and I would no longer be working at Bloomfield College. Upon trying to get the right paper work I needed to apply for unemployment, my field manger and I got into an argument. I don't know if the sight manger ever contacted him, but he called me and told me that I was fired. In amazement I laughed to myself, not only did I have the money to furnish my trip but I was now going to receive unemployment while I was in West Virginia. I thought it was the greatest thing in the world.

Back at Mrs. Thompson house things weren't getting any better. On several occasions I caught Jeffery's girlfriend talking about me to one of the children. Since they were kids they didn't know how to read lips without making any facial expressions. So I always knew when they were talking about me. I didn't let it bother me anymore because I knew I was leaving and I wasn't going to tell them until a few days before my bus was to leave. I vowed that I would never ever move back to Paterson no matter what I had to do to survive.

A week or so when I was about to leave I told Mrs. Thompson that I was leaving, she told me to make sure that that's what I wanted to do. I let her know that I bought my ticket and I was leaving within the next few days. When it was time to leave I put my T.V and DVD player in a big blue Tube, to make sure the tube didn't open I put a lot of grey tape around it. I also put all of my cloths in the same kind of tube. Since Jeffery and Victor got into a heated argument a few weeks before I was about to leave, Mrs. Thompson would not let Victor into the get to help me.

I thought that was so pretty petty, she knew the tubes were heavy she made me carry them all the way out of the gate. Instead of her saying go ahead and help Krystal but don't start any trouble she started screaming at Monica I don't want him in my gate. Monica tried to explain Mrs. Thompson those tubes are heavy. She said, "I don't care I don't want him inside of my gate."

I couldn't wait to get on the bus and out of New Jersey, no matter what Mrs. Thompson and Robert may say they showed exactly how much they cared about me. Yes they allowed me to stay but deep down inside they didn't want me to and their actions showed all the time.

Once I got to West Virginia I felt like a weight had been lifted off of my shoulders I was able to breathe again. I had my own privacy, I didn't have to walk around wondering if this or that person was talking about me. I was able to sleep stress free. After I got situated in my room I was told that the café was close for the summer and I would have to fin for my self. Since I had my unemployment and food stamps I wasn't too worried about how I was going to eat. I switched my unemployment checks to direct deposit so I wouldn't have to worry about how I was going to get the checks out of the mail.

Just as I started to relax and let my hair down, things started to go sour. One day when I went to buy food from the corner shop my food stamp card was denied. Upon calling the one eight hundred number, I was told someone called and stopped my benefits. I knew it was bullshit because no one knew I was receiving food stamps and no one had my social security number. Social Services stopped my benefits because I was using my card in another state. Since I didn't have my food stamps any more I was forced to use my unemployment checks for food and any and everything else I needed.

Because I didn't have a refrigerator I would always buy just enough food to last for a few days and crack my air conditioner up to make my room as cold as an ice box. I bet you're wondering why she didn't just buy a refrigerator. To be honest I don't know. Maybe I just was young and dumb. I knew that I needed a work-study job so I applied for a job at student life. After a few days I was given a job by Stacey and Malik Williamson. They job was pretty easy all I had to do was stuff envelopes, but I didn't have the job for long. Around August I went back to New Jersey to stand for court in front of the judge.

I was blessed when the judge dropped every charge but the dui; the entire time the judge was talking I was standing praying asking God to get me out of this situation. I ended up with a six month suspension, doing a two day dui class and close to about seven thousand dollars or more in fines. I wasn't too worried about the fines, I was just thanking God the judge dropped all the criminal charges against me.

Don't get me wrong seven thousand dollars is a lot of money but I knew that the criminal charges would stay on my record forever.

Chapter 20

Shearmark

*W*hen I arrived back to work, Malik told me I was fired. I didn't sweat the lost of the job; I just looked at him and smirked. School was about to start so I knew there would be plenty of jobs available. I just needed to find one.

While looking for a job I remembered delivering a package, to two funny and attractive women down in the Cougar Den, Isabella & Rachael. Why not try there, what did I have to lose? After talking to her she was glad to give me a job, after all she needed the kitchen help but informed me I couldn't start until I got a hat to cover me hair. After a few days Isabella decided that she would find me a hat herself because she really needed me to work. Everyone was cool down in the den.

Kelvin the head cook had been working in the den for a few years. Isabella asked him to show me around the kitchen and show me how everything was done. I explained to him that I had never worked in food service before and I really didn't know what was expected of me.

Little by little I started to introduce myself to everyone. I met Sharonda who was the head cashier she was cool as shit and very down to earth. Terry who I had already known from the year before was also cool, but everyone know that Terry did his own thing. He had his own schedule. Then there was this girl name Jessica. She was also pretty cool but she kind of stayed to herself and never really talked much. Keith who was a student had been working there for about two years or so he was a little wired but at the same time he was still cool. There was a girl by the name of Kima who had been working there for a few years. She was cool and she helped me get the swing of everything.

Last but surely not least it was this older woman by the name of Tia. Tia got on each and everyone's nerves, nothing you did or said was ever good enough.

She would always bitch or complain about the least thing. Working in the den was really hard to get used to. Several students started out with me but at the end of three or so weeks it was only me and this girl named Jessica that lasted. Working in the den was very stressful especially since some of the students were ass hoes. Plus having a bad temper wasn't helping.

One day while planning a catering event for a wedding, the entire kitchen started to attack each other. Victoria was taking a students order, and I guess the student didn't like what he or she received so they went to Sharonda like always.

Most students looked at Sharonda like a mother so they would always come to her anytime they had a problem. If she wasn't able to help, she would report the problem to the boss. This particular day Sharonda went to Victoria. Victoria responded with an attitude which ticked Sharonda off, next thing you know they're arguing back and forth. Over on the kitchen I was starting to argue with Tia. She was yelling and screaming saying I didn't make a student's order right.

Keith decided to run up the hill to the church where the bosses were to inform them of what was happening. Isabella, who was the Food service director and head boss, ran down the hill and stormed into the kitchen from the back door. Isabella under frustration with the wedding starting to scream and yell asking what the hell is going on.

Everyone just kind of looked at each other for a second. After two or three minutes of quietness Sharonda started telling Isabella what was gong on with her and Victoria. Isabella then stated you're the cashier; you have no reason to be back here in the kitchen. She then looked at me and side whose next I tried to calmly explain what was going on but my temper got the best of me. And before I knew it I was punching on the metal table in the kitchen.

Isabella's face in shock turned a blood shot red and started screaming you want to bang on my table get out your fired. I knew because of all the fines I had to pay, I really needed the job. No matter how pissed off I was I needed to talk to her and I needed to talk to her fast. I started walking behind her like Isabella wait let me explain something.

Chapter 21

Don't Mix Business With Pleasure

I guess even though she wanted to fire me, deep down inside she liked me as a worker. Next think I know Isabella told me to step into her office. I explained to her that I had a really bad temper and when I get upset the only way I know who to express my anger is punching walls or what every is around me.

She looked at me and said, "I understand you might have a bad temper but you need to learn a better way of dealing with your anger and your problems." It seemed like at least once every two weeks Isabella would fire and hire me all in the same day. If Isabella wasn't screaming your fired I was screaming I quit. I would call Debbie and say guess what Isabella or Monica did, I feel like quitting. Deb would always say, "Kris it's up to you, if you want to quit then quit." If not, take your ass back to work. No matter what happened in the den, I know I wasn't going to quit, I had too many fines to pay and a small window to pay them in. Pretty soon the bosses knew I wasn't going to quit either.

Even though I moved back to West Virginia to finish school, most of the time I would work, instead of going to class. One, I love making money and two I needed to gather as much money as possible to pay all my fines and surcharges. Some days when the den was short handed or during a lunch rush, Isabella or Monica would call me and Jessica while we were in class to see if we would come in and help for a few hours.

Jessica would always say, "Yes, depending on what her class schedule was like". As for me whether I had class or not I would still come to work. Most of my teachers were cool. They knew I worked in the den, so I would either bring them lunch or coffee the next time I was in class.

Since Jessica and I had worked so hard, Isabella decided to hire us as a part time Shearmark employe. With me being a Shearmark employee I was able to use my work-study elsewhere on campus. Brook, one of the resident assistant students I was friends with, helped me get a job in the dorms signing guest in and out of the building. There is a saying, "You should never mix business with pleasure, and man do I wish I would have listened."

A few hours before the New Year of two thousand and six, Brook and I got into a big argument. She was in her room lying down, sick with a cold or the flu, while I was in the hallway talking and hanging out with a few friends.

To make a long story short, Brook came out of her room yelling and screaming saying, "You guys are talking to loud go to your rooms." And of course I wasn't going to let her get away with talking to me like child. Before you knew it we were standing in the middle of the hallway arguing back and forth. Little did I know that argument would lead to, several life changing events.

A few nights later while I was on shift at the front desk talking to a few friends, a gentleman passed by me walking extremely fast, so I didn't get the chance to stop him and sign in. Within the next few minutes Brook comes down stairs trying to embarrass me in front of my friends saying, "You were supposed to stop him and sign him in". If you can't do the job then let me know and I will find someone who can. When she walked away that comment stuck in my head. Ten to fifteen minutes later, I walked to her room and gave her the sign in sheet. I said, "You told me if I couldn't do the job then let you know, well hell I'm letting you know I can't do the job."

The next school day, the housing director called me into her office and said, "I need to talk to you." Since Brook was sitting in her office pretending to be busy, I already knew what it was. She said, "Krystal, things are not working out with you working for me so I'm going to have to let you go." I just looked at her and said, ok and walked away.

Just a few weeks later it was my mom's birthday so I was in the dorms drinking with a few friends and celebrating. I even knocked on a few friends' doors to see if they wanted to take a birthday shot with me.

While I was going door to door taking birthday drinks, one of my underage friends and her girlfriend asked could they hang out in my room and watch TV. Me being the cool cat that I am I said, "Sure, just make sure when you finish you just close my door." An hour later after I returned to my dorm room, I noticed the bottle of liquor I had in my room was almost gone. I didn't sweat it, I figured it was late; I would approach them tomorrow and make them replace it.

Chapter 22

I Can't Win For Losing . . . .

*B*efore I could get into a deep sleep, one of the on duty RAs came knocking on my door. She asked, "Did you give so and so and her girlfriend liquor". I replied no, and said, "They asked could they watch movies in my room and when I retuned I noticed my bottle of vodka was low." I also stated you can ask anyone, I wasn't even in my room. I was upstairs having drinks with a few friends; she said ok then closed my door.

No more then 30 minutes later, a different RA knocked on my door and said, "The students told them, they received the alcohol from me." Brook the RA I use to be cool with said, "She witnessed me asking people to take a birthday shot with me." I tried to explain, "Yea I did ask some people to take a birthday shot, but I didn't ask them." For the simple fact, they were under age and always trying to hurt themselves. Next thing I know, at 2'oclock in the morning the Beckley Police Department was knocking on my door asking to see my Id and asking me questions.

Since I had a dui in New Jersey, I was afraid the Police would try an arrest me on those grounds. Since I didn't have any family in WV, the only person I knew to call was Isabella. Even though she was my boss at times she was there for me like a parent. That particular night she picked up the phone and said, "Kris they can't arrest you for having alcohol problems in New Jersey." I called Isabella back a second time, because one of the officer's was really nasty and tried to insinuate he was coming back to arrest me. When I called her back the second time she said, "Kris your fine and you better not call me again unless you're in jail."

The police never did a follow up. They actually understood that I did not physically give the girls alcohol but by the university standards I would be held accountable for leaving them in my room unattended. That next morning I was told I had to see Malik Williamson who is now the dean of students. Malik told me he spoke to several students that said, "Yes I was going around asking different students to take drinks." Why should he believe these two girls did not receive the alcohol from me? He said, "Even if I didn't physically give them the alcohol." I was still held responsible because no one is supposed to be in your room unattended.

He asked some of the RA's do they believe I would give alcohol to minors and one of them actually replied yes, and of course we all know that that RA was Brook. I was told I had to move out of the dormitory immediately, and I would not be able to register for classes next semester without taking alcohol counseling classes. After hearing this news I didn't know what I was going to do. I've looked for an apartment for some time now, and had no luck. I didn't know what I was going to do.

I did the only thing I could think of. Go down to the den and talk to mommy Isabella. Isabella just looked at me and said, "Kris it's not the end of the world." Months, weekends even days from now your going to look back at this college experience and laugh. Maybe Isabella had a point but I definitely wasn't laughing now. With all the bullshit I went through in NEW JERSEY there was no way in the world I was moving back.

Chapter 23

Talking to God . . . .

$\mathcal{F}$rom all of the stress I bought a pack of cigarettes and sat in the back of the dorm parking lot talking to myself and God. I just couldn't believe everything I went through to get back to WV would all be in vain.

Taking my last pull on the cigarette I looked up towards the sky and said, "God I know you didn't bring me this far to leave me now." I felt like why; would God bring me all this way, just to go through more trials and tribulations. I could have stayed in NEW JERSEY for all of this. It was getting closer and closer to the day I had to leave school property. Feeling hopeless I sat down at Rachel's desk and began to write a suicide letter.

In my letter I explained that I was tired of struggling, every time I took a step forward I would always take two or three back. No matter what steps I made to better myself, things always got worse as time went by. Even though I would miss my family it just seemed like the only way out. I was so grateful for so many of the faculty and staff members that tried to make WV feel like home, but it was time for me to take my life time card and clock out. With things so busy in the den I forgot to take my suicide letter when I went back to my dorm room.

That next morning Isabella and Rachel sent Terry to my dorm room to get me. They found my suicide letter in Rachel's desk, and were afraid I might harm myself. Mr. Williamson told me since I was a suicide risk he wanted me to leave the dorms immediately like today. Rachel told me if I wanted, it would be ok to say with her for a few days.

I really appreciated her letting me stay with her family, but I still hadn't found a place to stay. Most of the places I found weren't even remotely decent, or they wanted eight hundred dollars or more to move in.

One of the guys that I was cool with mentioned what about moving into with the girl that got drunk in your dorm room. Even though I thought it was a crazy ideal, he explained how else, are you going to come up with the money you need to move into a descent place. I really didn't want to move with Melissa but I really didn't have any other choice. Working at the den I wasn't making a lot of money, so I knew I was going to need a roommate.

I contacted Melissa, and said, "Since you had to move out of the dorms also would you like to move in together and be roommates". She totally agreed. I mean how else was she going to afford her own apartment? She was a college student for god sakes. After searching high and low, Melissa and I finally found a nice two bedroom apartment that was reasonable, but none of the utilities was included. We even had to pay for trash. The Landlord wanted eight hundred dollars to move in and neither one of us had four hundred dollars.

After some convincing, the landlord finally agreed to let us move with the terms of paying 400 this week and 400 within the next two weeks. Isabella feeling concerned called and said, "Kris I just received my taxes back, if you want I can loan you a few hundred dollars, just pay me back little by little." I told Isabella I appreciated her trying to help me, but Melissa and I got up all the money we needed to move in.

Chapter 24

The New Apartment

R ight after Melissa and I moved in Kima came over to the station where I was working and asked me for my house keys. When I got home later on that evening I saw Isabella had brought me a bed comfort, some items for the kitchen and bathroom. She also brought some kind of door sign that said girly girl which she knows darn gone well that was a lie, and she also brought me a sign that said drama queen.

Shortly after moving in, Melissa started falling behind on her half of the bills. Whenever I would ask for her half of the rent, she would always say oh I mailed my half in. Anyone could clearly see that she was lying. Why would a person just send part of the rent? That was the dumbest lie I ever heard. Why not just say my mom doesn't trust me with cash so she's going to send it straight to him.

Each and every month she would come up with a different excuse of why she didn't have her part of the rent. Our landlord was a much older man, so clearly I wasn't worried about being evicted until about two or three months later. One morning I received a knock on my door from a gentleman who looked like he was somewhere around forty or so. He said, "Hi my name is Zack; I am your new landlord." The first thing came to my mind; no way is this landlord going to let us go for rent being late or some months not paying at. I immediately phoned Melissa and said, "We need to start paying our rent at the beginning of the month." If each and every month I'm going to pay the four hundred by myself let me know and I will have Zack take you out of the lease and the apartment will be mine and mine alone.

The very next month when it was time to pay rent Melissa disappeared and went to Charleston with her girlfriend. I tracked her down and said, "Melissa this isn't fair every month I'm paying rent and all the utilities by myself, yet and still you live here." If by Monday you don't have your half of the rent I'm calling Zack to see if he can file eviction papers to put you out, because I'm not busting my ass for nothing. I will find a roommate that will pay her half of the bills or I will do it by myself.

Sunday night I contacted Melissa and asked, "Did she remember our little phone conversation." She told me don't worry about eviction papers I'm going to stay with my girlfriend, just point my things to the side and I will come and get them soon.

I decided that instead of getting another roommate I would work as much over time as possible and keep the apartment to myself. Since the den would be closed for the summer I decided to get a summer job. There was no way in the world I would be able to pay all of my rent with unemployment check.

After about a month talking to different people on campus, I scored a job with maintenance. It was an okay job; it was just hot as hell. The summer of two thousand and six at the time was the hottest summer WV had ever seen. My job was to clean the Cougar Den after the kids who attended the MOUNTAIN STATE UNIVERSITY basketball summer camp finished eating. My job was also to clean the library and all the offices inside of the library. When the campus closed at the night, my duties were to lock the doors, clean the windows and vacuum the hallways. The entire process took six hours. It was a little rough at times but the pay was great, eight dollars an hour.

Chapter 25

New Addition

*J*ust before school was about to start Isabella decided to have a meeting with all employees discussing the different things that would be happening during the new fall school year. Just as we were able to end our meeting, she stopped and smiled. Oh by the way I'm pregnant and I'm due next February. Everyone looked at her in excitement and said, "Oh my god Isabella. Congratulations I'm so happy for you." I couldn't believe what she had just said. I felt betrayed. I felt left out. But no matter what I didn't show it, in my facial expression. After the meeting I decided to clean Rachel's office and told Isabella I wasn't going to clean her office.

Isabella just laughed thinking I was joking but I knew I was serious. When Isabella came back from lunch and saw I was joking about not cleaning her office. She was furious, her face turned as red as peach. After I left, I kind of felt bad. I didn't think Isabella would take it that serious. On my way home I phoned her in the office and said tomorrow I would clean your office plus mop and vacuum. She was excited at the thought of her office being squeaky clean.

With school starting back in August, I decided to keep both the maintenance job and the cougar den. There was no way in the world I would ever be late paying rent with two jobs. Working both jobs for the first a month was ok, financially it was awesome. The following month was hard to stay afloat; I would work the den from ten in the morning too seven at night. Then work maintenance from seven at night till two in the morning. Some nights I was so tired, I wasn't able to walk home. I would sleep in the maintenance closet and the next morning one of the students would give me a ride home to shower and change my cloths.

Soon it got to the point; I wasn't physically able to work both jobs. Some days when I would get to work Isabella and Rachel would look at my face and say, "Krystal go see someone in the nursing department. Your face is swollen really bad. Your blood pressure might be up." Most days when that happened, my blood pressure would be 200/178.

One day Isabella sat me down and said, "Krystal I love you working for me but there's no way in the world you can physically continue to work both jobs."

I asked her which one I should quit. She said, "You have to choose which job is financially better." Funny think is I didn't have to make a choice. One particular day I was running late cleaning the den, so I decided to clock in for my maintenance shift. That way I wouldn't lose any of my hours.

I few days later the maintenance supervisor pulled me over and tried to yell and scowl me about the incident. When the supervisor started yelling, I said, "Hold up, your not Isabella or Rachel." Don't think I'm going to stand here and let you scream and yell at me. It's not going down. He fired me on the spot and told me to return my uniform.

I told him I would return them when I had the time. If he wanted the uniforms, that bad he could pick them up from my house. The next morning Isabella called the kitchen while I was working and said, "The maintenance supervisor told her he was having problems with me and I wouldn't return my uniform." She told me to bring them in and return them tomorrow morning. Everyone on campus would always call Isabella or Rachel whenever there was a problem with me, like they were my mothers.

Chapter 26

Shearmark A Family

*P*eople fail to realize that we were a family in the den. Terry, Sharonda, Jessica, Kima, with Isabella being the mom and Rachel being auntie. When I first met Jessica we had a Forensic class together but we never really talked much. Since working together in the den Jessica and I along with her boyfriend had become more than friends. Some would probably say we were more like family. Around October or November our Cougar Den family started to change. Kima found a better job and quit but was replaced with an older lady by the name of Gloria.

For an older woman Gloria was cool as hell. Most of the students in the den called her mommy. A little while later Isabella fired Sharonda and replaced her with a cashier named Erica. Even though it was not the team I started with, we were still a family.

With the spring semester approaching, Isabella's due date started to get closer and closer. It seemed the closer it got the more annoying she became. Everyone would laugh while Isabella and I literally argued standing in the middle of the kitchen.

Rachel would laugh and say, stop arguing with your mother before you make her go into premature labor. I would always get mad and storm off saying, you guys don't understand. It seems like she fucks with me just to piss me off. A few weeks after school started I helped Rachel throw Isabella a huge baby shower in the Cougar Den. Since the baby shower was during work hours Jessica and I really didn't get a chance to enjoy our self, until the students starting leaving one by one.

That next week Isabella sat everyone down and explained the den was going to stay open until seven thirty or eight from now on. Most of the students were complaining. The den closed way too early. They were paying for a meal plan they weren't using, especially if they had a late class. Since I needed the money, I told Rachel and Isabella I wouldn't mind staying until close. The first night we were open late was a memorable moment, the morning before or the day before, the little general store in Ghent West Virginia exploded.

Since it wasn't going to be any bosses working at night Carlos, Jessica's boyfriend called in and asked, "Did I want him to bring some liquor, when they came back in the den to watch American Idol." I looked at the phone in excitement and screamed hell yea why not.

After we closed at eight Jessica decided to drive around, since no one was ready to go home. That night we drove through Ghent to see the scene where the gas tank exploded and burned down the little general store.

The next few weeks I had so much overtime, I was barely able to stand at the cash register.

Chapter 27

Accident That Changed My Life . . . .

One late Tuesday night while I was sleeping Rachel called, but I didn't answer. I knew she was calling me to come in earlier then twelve in the afternoon. Instead of calling Rachel I called Jessica instead. I asked, "Did Rachel call you?" Jess said, "Yes but I didn't answer and I'm not calling her back." The snow is too bad for me to be driving.

As I looked at my phone, debating whether or nor I should return Rachel's phone call, a cold chill came over my body. At the same time, a voice in my head came saying over and over do not call her back.

Knowing I needed the money I quickly phoned Rachel back. She told me Terry was sick, she needed me to cover his shift of seven in the morning till two in the afternoon as well as my regular shift. I said, "No problem I would be in at seven. I immediately called Jess back to let her know I was working Terry's shift. Jessica wanted to come and get me, so in the morning I would be a little closer to the school, and would have far to walk.

I told her don't worry, I didn't mind the walk, I was used to walking by now. My alarm clock woke me up at around five thirty or so. Even though I have walked to work on several different occasions, I felt there was something different about this walk. As I began to walk down my hill and turn unto Robert C Byrd Dr, I felt a cold chill run through my body again. For some odd reason I remember saying to myself, I'm not going to make it to work today. I don't know why I felt like that, but for some reason I did.

About thirty or so minutes into walking, I felt a sharp pain in my left foot and immediately afterwards I felt like someone hit me in the face with a rock.

The next thing I remember is falling to the ground in so much pain. I didn't know what was going on or what had happened. I heard a woman screaming, oh my God she was just walking on the side of the road, and that truck came out of nowhere and hit her. Before I knew it someone was standing over me asking, honey is there anyone I can call to let inform that you were involved in an accident. The first thing I thought of was my job, letting them know I would be unable to cover my shift.

After that I immediately gave her Jessica, Isabella and Rachel's number. I knew Jess would answer but I wasn't sure if Isabella or Rachel would answer.

Most times they would let the call go to voicemail, then return your call depending if it was important or not. For some unexplained miracle Rachel and Isabella picked up on the first ring. The woman who witnessed the accident told them I was walking down Robert C Byrd drive and I was hit by a truck.

I really don't remember what happened next, on the way to the hospital I was in and out of consciousness. While going in and out of consciousness, I remember telling Isabella and Rachel I wouldn't be able to come to work today but I'll be there tomorrow. They just laughed and said awl poor baby don't worry about work. It'll be a while before you actually step foot back into the kitchen. Jess and Carlos were with me the entire time I was in the hospital. Carlos told me from all the medicine they were giving me, every twenty or so minutes I would wake up yelling or blurting out crazy comments.

He said at one point I would wake up and start talking and right in the middle of the conversation I would fall asleep. Whenever I would wake up, I would pick up exactly where I would leave off. Jess was a God sent, she went through my cellular phone and contacted Debbie and Monica to explain everything that had happened

Once I was put into a room and the medicine started to wear off, I realized my injuries were more serious then I realized. The bones in my left foot and ankle were completely shattered; I would have to have some kind of surgery to reconstruct all the bones in both of them.

From the impact to the face my right eye socket was completely swollen shut. I also broke the bone in my lower eye socket. Later after I got situated in my room I started calling different family members and friends to let them know I was in a bad accident but I was still alive and kicking.

What's actually weird the same day I had my accident is the same day Anna Nicole Smith died, February 8, 2007. I called Monica and Debbie to find out when they were coming down to West Virginia to see me. Monica said it would be best for them to leave Friday morning to get to me Friday night.

Chapter 28

Hospital Stay

*S*ince I had no family in WV everyone took turns coming to see me, even staying the night. Jessica and Carlos stayed the first night. Erica stayed with me the following night. So many of my friends and students from MOUNTAIN STATE UNIVERSITY came to see me and spent a couple of minutes with me almost each and every night. A few of them brought flowers, cards even balloons. Someone even brought me condoms that were made to look like flowers; I thought that was kind of cool.

Since I didn't like the hospital food, Gloria, Erica, Jess and Carlos took turns bringing me food from the den. Monica, Debbie and Monica's new boyfriend Walt came to see me Saturday, but didn't make it in time to see me before the surgery. Jess and her mom walked along side of my hospital bed as the nurses wheeled me down to surgery. It's a little odd but I remember the surgeon trapping my arms down to the time giving me a shot, then telling me to slowly count backwards from 20.

Next thing I remember is waking up in so much pain, begging the nurse to give me something for pain and it wasn't normal pain it was a knife stabbing, throbbing pain. I just remember begging please, can you give me something else for the pain. The nurse just looked at me with this pitiful face, and said honey, "I'm sorry I can't give you anything else. You're going to have to wait until your medicine kicks in, and it should be kicking in pretty soon."

It seem like, the medicine took for every to start working. Once I made it back up stairs to my room, Debbie Monica and Monica's boyfriend was there waiting on me. Monica screamed oh my God in disbelief; look at your face poor baby. Debbie was trying to play it and off said nah, it's not that bad Monica, but it was.

Monica took pictures of my face so just in case while I was working on the lawsuit I needed my lawyers to see how bad my face was. My face looked just like Kanye West's face when he was involved in his accident.

Debbie and Monica were only able to stay for the weekend, since they both had to work the following Monday or Tuesday. The Following Monday I was alone. Since Valentines Day was coming, Isabella had everyone in the den making different dishes for the Valentine's Day event in the Cougar Den.

One day I found myself calling Isabella crying, begging and pleading asking would she let Jess off of work. Just so she could come and spend some time with me at the hospital. Isabella said, "Now Kris, I know you're lonely, maybe even down and out but I really can't afford to let Jess off right now". We're already short handled with you in the hospital. I really need Jess to work, let me finish some things and I will come up and see you.

Isabella said, "Kris I know that right now it feels like it's the end of the world, but everything happens for a reason." Right now you might not know what that reason is but sooner or later you will see and understand. Is there anything you need or want, maybe I should bring some magazines for you to read. Kind of jokingly she said, "Do you read ebony and started laughing out loud." She said, "No seriously all jokes aside I will bring you something to read and maybe something to put on your face, to help it heal so you won't have permanent scares later in life."

When Isabella came to see me, she brought me a magazine who wrote a story about her and her husband Benny. The story talked about their hardship of being a new couple, expected their first child and all the while Benny was stationed in Iraq fighting the war. Isabella also bought a little angel teddy bear that I still have till this day.

Chapter 29

Released From The Hospital

*A*fter being in the hospital for a little close to a week, one of the nurses said honey since you don't have any insurance the only walking aid we can release you with is crouches.

I looked at her in disbelief and said, "Man you have to be joking. Do you know how difficult it is, trying to balance close to three hundred pounds on one foot, thanks but no thanks." I figured maybe someone at the school would be able to get me a wheel chair or something. Even though I was ready to leave the hospital, I was so afraid of being home alone. Monica and Debbie wanted me to move back to New Jersey, so I would have them to take care of me.

The thought of hanging with Debbie, Monica and the rest of the family sounding pretty cool, but I knew my sisters had their own situations that they were going through or handling. I didn't want to add to their list of problems.

I was released from the hospital Valentines Day, Eric who I met at MOUNTAIN STATE UNIVERSITY four years ago, said he would meet me at my house and help as much as he could. Even though Eric and I met when we were attending MOUNTAIN STATE UNIVERSITY, we were more than friends, we were like family. Eric helped me into the house rearranged everything, so I would be able to sleep in the living room instead of in the bedroom. Even though Eric had his own life and family, he was always there when I needed him. There were days, when Eric had to work until twelve o'clock in the morning. He would check on me before work, on his lunch break. Sometimes if he wasn't too tired he would come and see me even after work.

The first night, being home from the hospital was a complete nightmare, a few hours after Eric went home I needed to go to the bathroom. Since I didn't have anything to assist me with, I had to think fast how I was going to get to the bathroom. The first bathroom run, I decided to hop on one foot, even though the bathroom was only around the corner, it took so much of my energy I decided I needed a different approach. My second bathroom run, I decided to squat down and slide on the floor until I made it commode. I use the bathtub to pull myself up on the toilet seat.

Even though this idea was a lot better it was pretty gutsy since I received stitches on my butt I from the accident.

Thursday morning I called one of the ladies from MOUNTAIN STATE UNIVERSITY, who told me to phone her if I needed anything.

I asked was there any way she could get me a wheel chair. She said, "No and stated laughing, my mom has a walker if you want it's yours." At first I thought she was playing until Eric to meet her at the college and she literally gave him a walker that older people use. At first I kind of laughed in disbelief, but once I started to use it, I found it was easy to maneuver and get around with.

The next morning Rachel came over to my house with groceries her and her mom bought, so I wouldn't have to worry about cooking or buying groceries. Even though Isabella was about to go on maternity leave, she stopped by and told me to make a grocery list with different things I wanted to eat, that would be easy to cook.

After everyone went grocery shopping Jessica and Carlos came over to the house and made sandwiches, bags of cookies and chips. So I would be able to grab what I wanted or needed without standing in the kitchen to long. To be funny Isabella grabbed the bottle of vodka I had laying on the floor, and put it in the cupboard so I wouldn't be able to reach it. Every night some of the college students would come over to play card games, or just to talk and keep me company.

Chapter 30

Survival

*T*he following Monday morning Eric came over to the house, to take me to my doctor's appointment in Charleston. Even though I really needed to go, we were both dreading the ride because Eric's license was suspended. Half way to Charleston a police officer pulled us over and asked for Eric's license, registration and insurance. Eric explained Sr. my license is suspended but I'm talking my friend to an eye doctor in Charleston she was just released from the hospital last week due to a bad accident.

The officer looked at me and said, "Sorry to hear that but I'm going to have to tow your vehicle. You can get it back today if someone who has a valid driver's license comes to get it." Once we arranged for one of Eric's friends to pick up the car, we decided the best thing us to do was reschedule my doctor's appointment for an area in Beckley.

Since I didn't have food stamps yet there were times, I would run out of food and have to send Eric to pick up food from the Cougar Den or have Jessica or Carolos bring me food when ever they would get out of class. Even though everyone would always say, "Kris Just call me if you need anything." I didn't feel comfortable depending on people or calling Rachel or Isabella at the drop of a hat. Especially since Isabella just had her baby, I know the last thing on her mind was me or work.

After a month being home from work started driving me crazy. I wasn't used to staying home or not being on the go. Eric would take me to his friend's house, or sometimes his cousin house, just to keep me from going in sane. Depending on the person's house it was sometimes difficult for me to get around. For example, Jessica's house had a lot of outside stairs for me to climb even before we got inside of the apartment. Once inside her apartment the bathroom was all the way to the back of the house. Anytime I was at her house I would never eat or drink too much.

I know it would be a task getting back and forth to the bathroom. Even if I did, I would try my best to hold it until I got home.

From me not working and having any income coming in, my bills were started to pill up. My landlord was pretty understanding he told me don't worry about rent he would never dream of putting someone in my predicament out. As for my utilities that was a whole nothing story.

My water and sewer bill were about a month or two over due, and were threatening to shut my water off. Even if I paid the water bill, the sewer company shut my water off.

Eventually my water and sewer were shut off. Since I had food stamps, Eric would buy jugs of water so I would be able to flush the toilet. A few days after my water was shut off, I received a disconnect notice form the electric company. After a few days of Eric telling me no matter how much pride you have, if these people want to help you let them. Are you really willing to sit home in the dark without water because your pride won't let you ask or take money from them?

A few days after calling my beastie from MOUNTAIN STATE UNIVERSITY my water, sewer and electricity bill was paid, but I knew I had to get on the ball with my lawsuit, I could not continue to live like this. Jessica called and told me there was a commercial on television stating it would lend cash to anyone who has a pending lawsuit. After careful consideration I called my lawyer to explain I can't live like this. Something needs to be done.

He understood, I needed the money, but wanted to do a background check just to make sure it is a legit company. If this company was willing to loan me money then go for it. My lawsuit would take anywhere from three or more years to settle. Within a few days of calling my lawyer I was told we would be applying for a small loan through this company. He wanted to make sure my injuries were one hundred percent healed before we thought about settling.

After going back and forth to the doctor for a little over two or so months, he was very certain my foot healed and was ready to start the second surgery. My second surgery was schedule May four at six in the morning. Eric wasn't able to take me to the hospital, because he had an emergency at work. His boss called him in the night before, so he gave me money for a taxi and said call before you left the house and as soon as you got home from the hospital.

Chapter 31

Healing

I arrived at the hospital around four or so in the morning, not to clear what time, after feeling out all the necessary paper work I was placed in a wheel chair and taken up to same day surgery. It took them forever to get prep me for surgery. The first pregnancy test they took, some how got lost, so we had to do the entire process all over. I tried to tell them, there's no way in the world I'm pregnant. The nurse laughed and said, "Sweetie I have to follow hospital procedures."

Around nine thirty or so we were Okayed to begin surgery. I remember the entire process of my first surgery, but for some reason my second surgery I don't remember a thing. It's like I blacked out or something.

The nurse let me sleep for about an hour or so, and then told me I could call my ride to go home. I couldn't believe it, I was still a little dizzy from the medication they give me when they put me under, but they were going to release me. As I was being wheeled out of the elevator, I asked the doctor who did my surgeries. When could I start therapy, he looked at me laughed and said, "Why, do you really need someone to teach you how to walk? See you for a check up in a few weeks; make sure you get plenty of rest."

With my second surgery out of the way, I though I was on my way to a full recovery. When I saw my doctor a few weeks later, I kept screaming and asking when, could he take me off of medical leave to return back to work. He filled out my papers and told me I could return back to work by the end of May or early June. For some reason it never dawned on me. My foot would never ever be the same after my accident.

A few days after my surgery I received a letter in the mail, my loan was approved and the company would be sending the check priority mail to me within the next few days. I was so excited, at the thought of paying bills and sending Monica and Debbie money. Even though Eric, Jessica, Carlos, and a few other people would always come visit me to keep me company. I was so depressed. Anytime I would have spare money I would buy me a drink just to calm my nerves and to help me sleep.

When you're used to working and always being on the go, it's hard to sit home and do nothing. Once the check came in the mail, I immediately took it straight to the bank.

After the check cleared I sent Monica and Debbie a few thousand dollars, paid my landlord the money that I owed him, which wasn't much since he was using my spare bedroom as a tool shed. My rent was only

200 a month. I sent the state of New Jersey a few thousand dollars for my insurance surcharge fines.

Even though Eric didn't want any money, I gave his Grandmother the money I wanted to give him, so he would be able to fix his license. Eric said since my license was restored if I wanted his car I could have it. Laughing he said, "You need it more than I do, plus you can chauffeur me around for a change."

I took Jessica and Carlos out to dinner at their favorite restaurant. To show them how grateful I was for having them as friends, and thanks for everything, they had done for me.

I decided to do something a little more personal and special for Rachel and Isabella. I wrote a poem and asked one of my friends could them make me a plaque to inscribe the poem's on. They were both so happy. I swore I saw a few tears, at least from Rachel. Isabella wasn't a very emotional person and if she did find herself getting choked up, she would have walked away pretending they were some errands she had to run.

I was ecstatic about returning to work, Rachel had a wedding event to cater and since Isabella was still on maturity leave it would only be two of us handling the event. Rachel asked me if I was sure about returning back to work. She wanted me to know she and Isabella loved me and my job would always be here waiting for me, just be sure my body was up for the work. Within the first hour or so maybe even two, my foot started burning and throbbing like it was on fire.

I was forced to take multiply breaks just to rest my foot. I felt so bad for Rachel, She was always use to me taking everything from her and not letting her carry anything like I was a gentleman. They would always laugh and say, you know for you to be a woman you're the strongest woman I've ever met. Since I wasn't able to carry anything, Rachel told me to start on the dishes, so when the event was over, we wouldn't have much cleaning to do.

Once we finished the catering event, I started to question myself. Was I really ready to return to work, and could I still handle the day to day routine of working in the kitchen.

I wasn't sure if I was rather to return to work, but I sure know I needed a vacation after everything I've been through in the last few or so months. Without any hesitation I jumped on the next bus boarding north to Jersey.

Chapter 32

Heading Home

*T*he first thing we did when I got to New Jersey was go to Red Lobster. Monica and Debbie were so excited about me being in New Jersey, they decided to throw a big barbecue and invite the entire family Things were going smooth until everyone started running outside playing different water games. As bad as I wanted to jump up and play, I knew it wasn't possible. My foot was still healing from the surgery I had two month ago.

Before I knew it, I was breaking down crying. I couldn't believe how much my life had changed. Everyone started coming to me saying, "Kris you're be okay, your be back to our old self, before you know it"

Monica and Debbie decided they wanted to go shopping and asked if I wanted to come. I said sure. I didn't think my foot would be a major problem; normally my foot would only hurt when I would stand in one place to long. Just as we started to cover some ground, I had to keep stopping and resting because my foot started to hurt so badly. I sat down any and every place I could. I stayed in Jersey for about a week or so, and decided I was ready to go back home.

Since the bus ride back to West Virginia was longer then the ride to Jersey, I convinced Monica and her boyfriend Walt to drive me back to WV.

A little while after I got back to West Virginia, Eric decided he wanted to drive down to Myrtle Beach since he hadn't seen his family in such a long time. The ride down was long but it was beautiful, the same weekend we went down was bike fest. We figured it would be a whole lot cheaper if we just stayed with his sister.

We tried to walk down the strip, but it was so difficult with all the injuries from my foot. Instead of walking we decided to wait until night and drove up and down the strip just so we could get a good view of everything. With the week approaching, we both know it was time to leave, but neither one of us wanted to leave the bright and beautiful skies of Myrtle Beach.

When I got back to West Virginia, I made up in my mind when school start back in August I would definitely be back working in the cougar den. I did little small events here and there just to get my body back in tune with working, also to strengthen my foot so that come August I wouldn't have problem cooking or doing anything else in the kitchen. Isabella and Rachel started me off with little things, like cleaning the oven's and cleaning under the deli, home zone and pizza bars.

Since school was about to start I decided to take one more trip to New Jersey before beginning work. I've never drove to Jersey so I asked Eric if he wanted to tag along and help me drive. We jumped on the ride shortly after I got off work, and didn't arrive to Paterson till about one or two in the morning. Eric and I were supposed to stay upstairs with Debbie, but since we couldn't wake her, we stayed downstairs with Monica and her boyfriend Walt.

We talked with Monica and Walt till about three or four in the morning. Around 12 or so Debbie comes banging and knocking asking, "Why didn't we wake her up?" We said, "We tried you wouldn't wake your ass up." Eric has never been to New Jersey, so we decided to give him the grand tour. Since West Virginia doesn't have mega malls like New Jersey, we decided to take Eric to Garden State mall and Willobrook mall. After spending time with Monica Debbie and others in the family, Eric and I left Monday morning.

Chapter 33

Going Back to Work

 hen the fall semester started in August, students were so excited to see me back in the Cougar Den. Most wanted me to make a special sandwich or dish for them to eat. The first couple of months working back in the Cougar den was the hardest thing I have ever done in my life. As long as I stayed on my feet I was able to move around without being in pain. Any time I sat down to rest, my foot and ankle would swell so bad, making it impossible for me to walk. When it was time to close I would have to stop, ever so often to let my foot rest.

I felt bad for Jessica and Gloria; always having to finish my station, because I was unable to. There were many nights my foot and ankle would swell so badly, I had to lip back and from around the house because I couldn't walk. Some days my foot and ankle looked so bad I went to the hospital. Just to make sure there weren't further damage to my injury. Whenever I was in the emergency room, physicians would say, honey if you don't get off this foot you're going lose it. Meaning they would have to amputate and cut of my foot.

At times I felt Isabella and Rachel believed I was faking, anytime I complained my foot and ankle was hurting. Some mornings when I would get up for work I could barely stand. One day I drove to the emergency room, explained to the physician I was in so much pain and needed a day to rest. After reexamining my injuries he agreed. I was given a work excuse for three days off.

The next morning when I went to give Isabella my doctor notice, she sat me down and said, "Kris I know your foot gives you problems, but sometimes you use it as an excuse, any time you're pissed off at me and Rachel." Go home rest, stay off your foot so you can return to work without problems.

Around November or December, Debbie said, "She was tired of living in New Jersey and wanted something better." When Debbie moved, her boyfriend was so pissed the entire drive down he didn't say one word. He didn't say one thing until Debbie and I started playing. She said, "Kris you better watch your mouth don't make me pull your wig off in front of Mike."

I looked at her and said, "Please I'll take it off myself." Next thing you know I pulled off my wig and all you saw was my holy wig cap.

Mike looked at me and busted out laughing. Debbie paused looked at me and started laughing. She said, "Kris, you have no fucking shame."

Then when I tried to put the wig back on, it was turned sideways. Mike started laughing and said, "Deb that's your sister."

Once we arrived in West Virginia, Mike drove me to my car which was parked in MOUNTAIN STATE UNIVERSITY parking lot. The road was so bad from the snow; my car did a full three hundred and sixty degree spin before I was able to regain control. The move went pretty fast, what every items Deb wasn't going to use was put in storage.

Just when I thought everything in my life was good. My landlord informed me he would no longer be using my spare bedroom. Instead of paying two hundred dollars a month I would be paying four hundred. He said, "Someone bought our apartment complexes and the guy was a real asshole." Try not to be late with your rent if possible. I took Debbie different places to fill out job applications. Within a week of her moving in, the transmission in my car died. I knew no matter how bad things looked, they were only going to get worst.

After my car broke down it was hard getting back and forth to work. Isabella loaned me the work van and said, "Only use it to get back and forth to work. Don't have any one else in the van." Since my rent went from two hundred to four hundred dollars. It was beginning to be hard to pay my rent on time. Every month I would be a few days late. On top of that, I would only have enough for pay rent and not late fees. Summer only made things worse; I had to wait for two unemployment checks to pay rent instead of one.

The new landlord Jim called and said, "Kris I'm tired of you being late, I'm going to file eviction papers". Most people would have told me Kris it's not that big of a deal. I have never been taken to court to be evicted. To me it was a very big deal. After stressing for a day or two, I decided to grab me a drink. After my second or third drink, I decided I wanted to end my life. I was tired of struggling and barley making it. Every time I turn around something fucked up was happening in my life. I grabbed the pain pills that were on my dresser, it started taking them one by one.

Chapter 34

I Just Can't Take It Any More

*D*ebbie was in the living room watching television. She didn't know what was going on. Once I started filling dizzy and quezzy, I grabbed a pen and paper. I needed to write my suicide letter. I wrote a personal message to my biological family and a letter to my West Virginia family. Monica tired to call Debbie in the living room, since she wasn't responding she called me instead. Monica said, "Why does your voice sound so funny?" I just finished drinking a bottle of vodka and took several pain pills. Monica hung up with me and continued to call Debbie until Deb picked up. Within minutes Debbie busted through my door hung up with Monica and called 911.

The ambulance arrived and immediately drove me to a hospital that dealt with suicidal patience's. When I arrived at the hospital, the doctor asked Deb for my suicide letter. He explained were sending her to detox, and then keeping her for further observations. After the hospital gave me a few medications to offset everything I had taken, little by little I started waking up.

Within a few hours one of the doctors came to see me. He said, "Krystal we're going to keep you for further observations." I looked at the doctor smirked and said, "I'm walking out the door and theirs nothing you can do to stop me." He said, "Krystal, you're not leaving if we have to I will call security to restrain you. The only way you can leave, if your sister Debbie signs you out." Debbie looked at the doctor and said, "I don't wait her to start acting crazy, so yea I will sign her out."

The following Thursday, I went to court to appear before the judge to plead my case. I informed the judge, I had just been released from the hospital, due to a suicide attempt. She looked at me like she was saying to herself, ok what does that mean. After she looked at me I knew there wasn't anything I could have said to change her mind. Jim my landlord said, "I want her to pay late fees for the months she was late and I want her to move out." The judge gave me thirty days to vacant his property. Plus he wanted rent for thirty days I was staying there.

After I left court I felt a heavy weight had been lifted off of my shoulders. I looked at Debbie laughed, and said, "Do he really thing I'm going to move out and pay rent him?" What the fuck was he thinking?

He should have taken the money in court when I tried to give it to him. Now it's his fucking lost. I'm going to use the money to find another place. Debbie decided she was going to stay with one of our friends from school. For the first week or Two I stayed with Gloria at her apartment. Her boyfriend had his own house; therefore I was mostly at the apartment by myself. After the third week my friend Jennifer, a senior from MOUNTAIN STATE UNIVERSITY decided it would be a good idea for us to get an apartment together. I told Jennifer sure I didn't mind. I needed a place to stay some until an apartment came available at the complex I filled and application out with.

Even though I didn't like having a roommate Jennifer and I had so much fun. At the time Jen was dating one of the basketball players. Every evening after work we would pile in front of the television light a blunt, have a few drinks and play video games. Little by little I started having more and more problems with my foot. After work I would sit in a chair roll my self out of the Cougar Den and lip on one foot down the stairs and out to the car.

Once home I would call Jen to meet me outside so she could help me walk into the house. My foot was getting worst and not better. I decided to apply for disability. When I applied they informed me I would immediately be denied because I was still working. The following February I was notified by phone my apartment was ready, at any time I could move in. I told Jen I was moving but would still give her money for the electricity bill.

A few weeks before I moved Isabella told me she was resigning and a new boss would be taking over. The night I decided to move it started to snow. I called Eric to reschedule but he said non-sense lets do it now so we can get it out of the way. The apartment building I was moving into was right next door to Gloria. Some nights after work Gloria and I would be so worn out, soon as we walked through the door she would light a blunt, and I would pour the drinks.

Chapter 35

Making Me Happy

I ngrid the new boss saw how difficult it was for me to work with my injuries and decided to rearrange my schedule. She said, "Instead of working ten in the morning till seven in the evening every day. You can work six in the morning till seven in the evening and only have to work three days out of the week. It would also be every other day."

The schedule she mapped out for me was working beautifully for the first few months. One day when we returned from spring break, my foot swelled the size of a pineapple.

After work I immediately went to the hospital. The doctor who examined my foot thought it would be wise to stay off my foot for a few days. It looked really bad. He was afraid they might have to impute, if I didn't start taking better care of myself. The following week I returned to work, my leg started to swell again. Since it felt warm, my boss being alarmed told me to leave now and go straight to the hospital.

Instead of going to the hospital I made a doctor's appointment to see a podiatrist specialized. After doing several different test and x-rays he said, "Kris I'm going to release you from work. Your doctor should have never cleared you for work, no matter how much you begged him. April 13, 2009 I was placed on medical leave and told I could not return back to work.

Things were totally different this time off from work. After I received my medical leave papers I ran to the Cougar Den. I was so happy. I was tired of coming home each and every day limping around the house because my foot was swollen.

This time out of working I was going to enjoy myself. Two days after being put on medical leave I went to unemployment. Since I wasn't going to be working I needed income coming to make sure my rent and bills were paid and paid on time. Around May or June Kasey said, "Since he wasn't working, he was thinking about taking a trip to West Virginia to see me."

A few weeks later Kasey and his best friend Aunt Rita came down to WV. Kasey and Aunt Rita had never been to Beckley. They asked could I show them around so I gave them the grand tour. After showing them around, Kasey said, "Let's go out for a few drinks. It's not like we have to work in the morning. We ended up going to Fosters having a few drinks and reminiscing down memory lane.

The next morning while Kasey was sleeping, Aunt Rita and I decided to chat and play catch up. So many things changed since the last time we seen each other. While we were talking she asked, had I come out of the closet. I shook my head and said, "Auntie I'm not gay." Laughing she said, "Your in denial". She asked, "Have u ever been with a woman." I lied and told her no. Aunt Rita looked at me and said, "Kris you're lying, you and I both know you've been with a woman before." When you're ready, and realized, no matter what you do, you can't change who you are, people are going to love you no matter if you're straight or gay. I just looked at her and said, "Auntie I'm not gay." The truth is for years I struggled with my sexual identity.

Even when I was a small, I could see I was a different from most of the girls in our family. While everyone else was learning to play double-dutch, I was throwing my basketball up in the hair over power lines. One day while Auntie Latoya and Debbie was teaching my cousin Rebie and a few other girls from the neighborhood how to jump rope. They called me over and said, "Kris get in the middle of the rope we're going to teach you too."

After a few tries Auntie Latoya and Debbie got frustrated. They threw me ball and said, "Go ahead back and finish playing basketball. While other girls were in class talking and flirting with the boys, I would be on the other side of the table, trying to figure out what video games they had so we could trade.

Most little girls would ask for baby dolls for Christmas, so they could learn how to braid hair. Me, I always asked mom for whatever new video game was out at the time. Even if mom did buy a baby doll, I would write all of her face, and have the dolls hair so tangled mom would throw it in the trash. When I was younger, I had so many different video game systems mom decided she would rent a three bedroom apartment instead of two, so I could have my own game room.

When I was younger, while my mom was sleep I would tip-toe into Debbie's room put on her pant's and walk around the house pretending I was boy.

For years I secretly struggled with my sexual identity. I didn't want to be just gay. I literally wanted to be a boy. I always dreamed of being my mother's first born son. Maybe if I had been a boy, my life what have been different. My family was very religious, I knew as a child there was no way in they were going to except I wanted to be gay. I always had a low self-esteem. I felt I was pretending to be someone I wasn't.

My sister's would always try to get me to be a girly girl. Kris go get your nails done. Buy yourself a new wig, the one you have is looking old and worn out. The truth is, I didn't care about getting my nails and hair done. If it was up to me I would walk around like a boy in jeans and a nice shirt.

One late November night I woke up and said, "I'm tired of living the way my family wants me too." After several weeks of thinking how my family would react. I said, "Screw them." It's about time I start making Kris Happy. I don't live for them and do they live for me. If my family don't want to accept who I really him, then tough break, don't come around me when I'm in New Jersey and I won't come around you.

As for my friends, most of them had already known I was gay. They were just waiting for me to stop living my life to make everyone else happy and start making me happy. When I finally got enough courage, I called Debbie at 12 or so in the morning because I knew any later her minutes would not be free. I asked, "Debbie how would you feel if I cut my hair and started dressing like a boy." She said, "I wouldn't feel any way that's your dam hair." I guest Debbie was talking in her sleep and really didn't understand what I was saying, so a few hours later she called me back.

Deb said, "Kris did you call me last night about cutting off your hair and dressing like a boy." She said, "You can dress like a boy, but you still have to wear a dress to church." I laughed and said, "Deb I don't think you understand what I'm saying." She said, "Oh are you saying you're coming out of the closet." Kris, no matter what I'm going to love you. You're my sister and you have to do what makes you happy.

But remember whatever you do, do it big. Meaning if you cut you hair, don't slack. Make sure you use a good barber. Stay on top of your gear. Immediately after hanging up with me Deb phoned Monica. Every twenty or so minutes they would call or texting me. Did you get your hair? Send us a picture.

Even though Monica and Debbie sound calm over the phone, later on I found out they were both nervous. They were scared how I was going to look without having any hair. The funny thing is when I sent them the picture, they both called and said, "Wow Kris you look better as a boy." For a second I paused on the phone. Even though they didn't mean to, my feelings were a little hurt. They both laughed and said, "Kris you know what we mean. We're saying we like the way you look."

January I made a trip up to New Jersey. Before my trip, I phoned everyone. Deb, felt it was important to let everyone know I was fully out with my sexuality instead of popping up. Some family members took it better than I thought. They always had a feeling I was gay, but was never really sure. Some family member's wanted to ask questions, and preach to me. God said, "This." God said, "That." At the end of the day they realized, I didn't care what they thought or had to say because little by little everyone soon learned to accept it.

Coming out of the closet made me fell like a new person. Finally, I felt I was being true to myself. I started going out more, even started to date. For once in my life things were starting to look up. I decided to enroll into college for the next school semester.

September 2010 I enrolled into New River Community Technical College majoring in business and marketing. For the first time in my life I'm not walking around worrying, what this or that person has to say about me? I'm happy. I can say that with a smile.

I'm totally the opposite of who I was in high school. I'm confident in myself and in my studies. I interact more with my classmates and participant in school functions. I finished my first two semester of school on the Dean's list. I'm enjoying my life being free.

It's sad it took for me to start making myself happy in order for me to be happy. Look out for Kris Jones in 2013, I'm doing big things now and this is only the beginning.